培梅食譜
<II>

傅培梅 著

經典・傳承

跟隨母親從事食譜出版已近20多年，以前是母親主導出版方向，我負責行銷，近年則是我和大姐負責選定方向，大姐製作、我出版行銷，母親則是我們的最佳顧問，她總是給我們很多意見和想法，尤其是兩年前我們決定開始重新製作她的代表作——培梅食譜第一集時，更是勾起她對往事諸多的回憶，一部中國彩色食譜的出版史，常由她口中娓娓道來。

記得那段日子，大姐和媽媽討論著每道菜呈現的方式，70歲的她仍是精神奕奕的表現著對自己食譜的堅持。從她的堅持中我找到了食譜出版的路，它讓我了解每一道「食譜」都有它的特殊性，因為每個掌廚人，對於食材配料選擇的喜好，添加調味料份量的不同，造成相同菜名的菜，每每會有不同的味道，讓吃的人有不同的感受，也造就了每個食譜作者能有不同的風格與受到不同讀者的喜愛。

這本食譜在編排選題上和第一集有著顯著的不同，以食材來分類，依您在家中現有的材料，給您意見，看可以怎麼煮來吃，而選的做法保證讓您喜歡又回味無窮。當然這本食譜仍保有培梅食譜的傳統——有著詳細的解說，只要跟著步驟做，一定成功。

每道佳餚的製作完成，都包含著無盡的愛，希望您在為您愛的人烹調時，也可以感受到我們對您的關愛與用心。

培梅食譜第一集再版仍受到海內外讀者的喜愛，一年後我們又開始著手第二集的再版工作，期間母親因肝癌復發，經化療仍不敵病魔辭世，於是如何讓她的食譜能更廣泛的流傳下去，成為我們做子女的深責大任，期許自己能在最近的將來把母親的食譜，以新面貌一一呈現給喜歡她的讀者朋友，讓「傅培梅的味道」能繼續在每個家庭中流傳。

程顯灝

目錄

培梅食譜 <II>

經典・傳承 002

雞肉篇 010

012 生炸去骨雞
Deep-fried Boneless Chicken

014 檸檬雞片
Fried Chicken Slices with Lemon Sauce

016 雙冬扒雞翅
Braised Chicken Wings with Mushrooms

018 香酥雞
Flavored Crispy Chicken

020 石榴雞
Pomegranate Shaped Chicken

022 紅燒八寶雞
Stuffed Chicken with Treasures

024 辣子雞丁
Diced Chicken with Peppers

026 雞凍
Jellied Chicken

028 生炒雞鬆
Stir-fried Minced Chicken

030 雀巢雞丁
Stir-fried Chicken in Bird's Nest

鴨肉篇 032

034 鹽水鴨
Spiced Duck Cold Cuts

036 鍋燒鴨
Fried Duck Pan Cake

038 涼拌鴨條
Roast Duck Salad

040 汽鍋鴨塊
Steamed Duck in Yunnan Casserole

042 芋泥鴨
Mashed Taro on Crispy Duck

046 糯米封鴨塊
Steamed Duck Pudding

048 滷鴨
Braised Duck

050 薑爆鴨絲
Quick Stir-fried Duck Shreds with Ginger

052 脆皮八寶鴨
Crispy Duck with Stuffings

056 荷葉粉蒸鴨
Steamed Duck in Lotus Leaves

豬肉篇 058

060 砂鍋獅子頭
Stewed Meatballs in Casserole

064 宮保肉丁
Diced Pork with Dried Hot Peppers

066 荔甫扣肉
Molded Pork with Taro

068 京都排骨
Fried Pork Spareribs, Jingdu Style

070 豉汁排骨
Spareribs with Fermented Black Beans

072 蒜泥白肉
Sliced Pork with Garlic Sauce

074 金錢肉
Roast Coin Shaped Pork

076 珍珠丸子
Pearl Balls

078 蔥串排骨
Stuffed Spareribs with Brown Sauce

080 京醬肉絲
Stir-fried Pork with Bean Sauce

牛肉篇 082

084 家常小牛排
Beef Steak, Home Style

086 咖哩牛肉片
Sliced Beef with Curry Sauce

088 玉蘭炒牛肉
Sliced Beef with Broccoli

090 中式牛肉餅
Stewed Meatballs, Chinese Style

092 紅燒牛腩
Stewed Beef in Casserole

094 蔥爆牛肉
Quick Stir-fried Beef with Green onion

096 滑蛋牛肉
Scramble Eggs with Beef Slices

098 魚香牛肉絲
Stir-fried Beef with Hot Sauce

100 紙包牛肉
Paper-wrapped Beef

102 紅燴牛尾
Stewed Ox Tail, Chinese Style

魚肉篇 104

106 煙燻鯧魚
Smoked Fish

108 酥炸魚捲
Crisp Fish Curls

110 豉汁魚球
Diced Fish with Fermented Black Beans

112 鍋貼魚排
Fried Turreted Fish

116 紅燒划水
Braised Fish Tails in Brown Sauce

118 紅燒鰻魚
Braised Eel with Brown Sauce

120 咖哩魚片
Sliced Fish with Curry Sauce

122 豆豉辣椒蒸魚
Steamed Fish with Fermented Black Beans and Hot Pepper

124 糖醋魚捲
Fish Rolls with Sweet and Sour Sauce

126 白汁燴全魚
Steamed Fish with Cream Sauce

海鮮篇 128

130 子母蝦
Baby and Mother Shrimps

132 乾燒蝦碌
Sautéed Prawn with Tomato Sauce

134 西炸小蝦排
Deep-fried Shrimp Cutlets

136 蛋黃蝦
Prawns and Egg Yolk Sandwiches

138 紫菜蝦捲
Minced Shrimp Rolls

142 醋溜明蝦片
Deep-fried Prawns with Sour Sauce

144 大燴鮑片
Abalone with Assorted Vegetables

146 金鉤魷魚絲
Shredded Squid with Pork

148 燴墨魚花
Cuttlefish Salad

150 鴛鴦蝦仁
Stir-fried Lovers Shrimp

豆腐、蛋篇 152

154 蟹肉扒豆腐
Tofu with Crab Sauce

156 鍋貼豆腐
Sautéed Tofu Sandwiches

158 家常豆腐
Sautéed Tofu, Family Style

160 三鮮豆腐墩
Scallops, Ham, and Mushrooms with Steamed Tofu

162 魚香烘蛋
Egg Omelet, Sichuan Style

164 三色如意捲
Tri-color Egg Rolls

168 中式蛋包
Chinese Rice Omelet

170 什錦蛋派
Assorted Meat in Egg Pie

172 蝦仁蒸蛋
Shrimp with Steamed Egg

174 涼拌干絲
Dried Tofu Strips Salad

蔬菜篇 176

178 釀蕃茄
Stuffed Tomatoes in Brown Sauce

180 十錦涼菜
Chinese Salad, Rich Style

182 雞絨蠶豆
Minced Chicken with Lima Beans

184 扒金銀菇
Braised Two Kinds of Mushrooms

188 和菜戴帽
Stir-fried Vegetables Covered with Eggs

190 蟹肉焗菜膽
Baked Chinese Cabbage with Crab Sauce

192 羅漢齋
Assorted Vegetarian Dish

194 三層塔
　　Quail Eggs and Mushrooms with Vegetables
198 火腿冬瓜夾
　　Stuffed Winter Melon with Ham
200 麻辣豆魚
　　Bean Sprout Rolls with Chili Sauce

湯品篇 202

204 原盅燉什錦
　　Steamed Assorted Ingredients in Casserole
206 百花鵪蛋湯
　　Stuffed Quail Eggs and Shrimp Ball Soup
208 什錦鍋巴
　　Popped Rice with Sea Food Sauce
212 油條蠣黃羹
　　Oyster and You-tiau Potage
214 清燉銀耳牛肉湯
　　Beef Soup with White Fungus
216 海鮮砂鍋
　　Seafood Hot Pot
218 清湯雙捲
　　Soup with Double Rolls
220 蕃茄玉米羹
　　Tomato and Sweet Corn Soup
222 菠菜豆腐羹
　　Spinach and Tofu Soup
224 三鮮干絲湯
　　Chicken, Ham and Shrimp with Tofu Shreds Soup

麵食篇 226

228 菜包子
　　Steamed Pastries with Vegetables
230 花捲
　　Steamed Flower Shaped Rolls
232 糯米燒賣
　　Stewed Pork and Glutinous Rice Dumplings
234 燒餅
　　Baked Sesame Seed Buns

238 油條
You-tiau

240 廣州燴飯
Rice with Assorted Ingredients, Cantonese Style

242 翡翠炒飯
Fried Rice with Green Vegetables

244 山東大滷麵
Assorted Meat in Soup Noodles

246 北方炸醬麵
Noodles with Minced Pork and Bean Sauce

248 川味涼麵
Cold Noodles, Sichuan Style

258 八寶芋泥
Steamed Eight Treasures Taro Pudding

260 沙其馬
Sha-Gi-Ma

262 雞蛋撻
Chinese Egg Tart

264 芝麻鍋炸
Deep-fried Custard Pudding

266 糯米捲尖
Fried Sweet Rice Pastry

268 椰絲糯米球
Glutinous Rice Balls with Coconut Flakes

270 千層糕
Steamed Thousand Layers Cake

甜點篇 250

252 壽桃
Steamed Long Life Cake

254 花生糊
Sweet Peanut Cream Soup

256 豆沙芋棗
Fried Taro Dumplings with Sweet Bean Paste

雞肉篇

雞各部份之用途

一隻雞通常可分為雞胸、雞腿、雞翅膀、雞腳與脊背（又名雞架子）等部份。
1. 雞胸肉：肉嫩無筋，適宜炸、炒，可切為丁、絲、片及絨狀來烹調。
2. 雞腿肉：多筋，肉富彈性，適宜燒、燉、燜與炸食。
3. 雞翅膀：多筋且皮厚，又脆韌，宜煮、滷、燒、燉、炸食。
4. 雞腳：多皮，富膠質，且筋絡多，有韌性，適宜滷、燒、煨湯等用。
5. 脊背：全屬骨骼，只宜煮湯用。用雞骨煮湯時應先將雞骨斬剁成小塊，全部用開水燙泡半分鐘，撈出後再用冷水沖淨，置深口湯鍋中加入開水及蔥、薑少許，以小火燒煮1小時以上便成。

About Chicken

Chicken can be divided into the following parts: the breast, legs, wings, feet, and back bones.
1. Breast: Very tender. No tendons or sinews. Can be deep fried or stir fried. Can be diced, shredded, sliced, or steamed and torn into pieces.
2. Legs: A lot of tendons and sinews. Also has elasticity. Can be boiled, stewed, braised or deep fried.
3. Wings: A lot of tendons and sinews. Also has elasticity. Can be steamed, boiled, stewed, braised, and deep fried.
4. Feet: A lot of skin. Also has elesticity. A lot of tendons and sinews. Can be boiled in five spicy sauce and stewed.
5. Back: Most of it is bone. Can be used to make stock. First, cut it into small pieces. Dip the pieces into boiling water for 30 seconds. Remove and plunge into cold water. Put the chicken pieces in a large pan. Add hot water and a few pieces of Green onions and ginger. Stew the stock over a low fire for at least half an hour.

生炸去骨雞
Deep-fried Boneless Chicken

材料 >>
雞腿3支（或雞胸2片）、炸油5杯、蔥屑2大匙、麻油1/2大匙、油1/2大匙

醃雞料 >>
蔥2支、薑2大片、八角1顆、醬油3大匙、酒1大匙

淋雞汁 >>
醬油1大匙、糖1大匙、水2大匙

做法 >>
1. 將每支雞腿中之兩根長骨剔出（小腿下端之小骨節仍要留在雞腿中），再把雞肉有筋部份用刀輕輕斬切數下。
2. 將蔥、薑拍碎、八角切開，全部放在大碗內，加入醃雞料調勻。放下雞腿醃半小時以上。
3. 在鍋內將炸油燒得極熱之後，投下全部雞腿，用小火炸約1分半鐘至熟，撈出後將油再行燒熱一次，然後放下雞腿重炸10秒鐘（大火）。
4. 將雞腿撈出，瀝乾油後每支橫面切成5塊斜刀大片。整齊的排置在盤中，上面撒下蔥屑。
5. 在炒鍋內燒熱麻油及油後馬上淋到盤中蔥花上面，使蔥散發香氣。
6. 將泡雞腿所剩下之醬油汁和淋雞汁倒在鍋內煮滾，再澆到雞肉上面便可趁熱上桌。（可用生菜做配飾）

Ingredients
3 chicken legs (or 2 chicken breast)
5 cups oil for deep fry
2 tbsp. chopped green onion
1/2 tbsp. sesame oil
1/2 tbsp. oil

To marinate chicken
2 slices ginger
2 stalks green onion
1 star anise
3 tbsp. soy sauce
1 tbsp. wine

Seasoning
1 tbsp. soy sauce
1 tbsp. sugar
2 tbsp. water

Procedures
1. After removing the bones from the legs, score the stringy part with knife for a few times.
2. Crush the green onion, ginger, and star anise. Put them in a bowl. Add the marinades, mix thoroughly to marinate the chicken for at least half an hour.
3. Heat the oil in a pan to very hot, deep fry the chicken legs over low heat for about 1 1/2 minutes until done. Remove the chicken legs. Reheat the oil, deep fry the legs again over high heat for 10 seconds.
4. Remove the legs and drain. Cut each leg into 5 pieces crosswise. Arrange it on a platter. Sprinkle the chopped green onion over legs.
5. Heat two kinds of oil to very hot, pour it over the onion.
6. Pour the remaining marinade in a pan and add the seasoning sauce. Bring it to a boil. Then splash this sauce over the chicken legs. Serve.

雞肉篇
培梅食譜II

檸檬雞片

Fried Chicken Slices with Lemon Sauce

材料 >>
雞胸肉400公克、炸油4杯

醃雞片用料 >>
蛋黃1個、鹽1/3茶匙、酒1/2大匙、醬油（淡色）1/2大匙、白胡椒粉1/8茶匙、太白粉1大匙、水1大匙

沾雞片粉料 >>
太白粉6大匙、麵粉2大匙

綜合調味料 >>
新鮮檸檬汁4大匙、糖3大匙、清湯或水3大匙、鹽1/4茶匙、太白粉2茶匙、麻油1/2茶匙

做法 >>

1. 將雞胸肉去皮後，切成3公分寬，5公分長之大薄片，（先將肉放在冰箱中冷凍15分鐘比較好切）。在碗內先將醃雞料拌勻，再放入雞片輕輕調拌好，醃約10分鐘。
2. 用一個小碗，將綜合調味料全部調妥備用。
3. 將醃好之雞片，仔細沾上混合好的粉料，然後投入已燒至8分熱之炸油中，用小火炸約半分鐘，全部撈出，重新將油燒至滾熱，再將雞片投入，炸約10秒鐘，撈出排盤中，油倒出。
4. 另用1大匙油炒綜合調味料，見汁已濃稠時，淋下1大匙熱油，使其明亮，淋在雞片上，趁熱供食。

Ingredients

400g. chicken breast
4 cups oil for deep fry

To marinate chicken

1 egg yolk
1/3 tsp. salt
1/2 tbsp. wine
1/2 tbsp. light soy sauce
1 tbsp. cornstarch
1 tbsp. water
1/8 tsp. pepper

To coat the chicken

6 tbsp. cornstarch
2 tbsp. flour

Seasoning sauce

4 tbsp. fresh lemon juice
3 tbsp. sugar
3 tbsp. soup stock or water
1/4 tsp. salt
2 tsp. cornstarch
1/2 tsp. sesame oil

Procedures

1. After removing the chicken skin, slice it into 3 cm~5 cm. Marinate for about 10 minutes.
2. Mix seasoning sauce in a small bowl.
3. Coat the chicken with the mixed powder. Deep fry it in 160°C oil over low heat for about 1/2 minute until golden. Drain and reheat the oil to very hot. Deep fry the chicken again for 10 more seconds. Drain and remove to a platter.
4. Heat another 1 tbsp. of oil to stir fry the seasoning sauce, when it become boiled and thickened, splash 1 tbsp. of hot oil to make the sauce shining. Pour the sauce over the fried chicken slices. Serve hot.

 盤邊可飾以檸檬片和香菜，蕃茄花之類，以增美觀，如喜食較酸者，可將檸檬片擠汁數滴於雞片上。
Garnish the platter with some sliced lemon and parsley. If you like more sour taste, squeeze some lemon juice over the chicken slices at last.

雙冬扒雞翅
Braised Chicken Wings with Mushrooms

材料 >>
雞翅膀10支、小冬菇10個、冬筍450公克、蔥1支、薑2片、香菜少許、炸油4杯

調味料 >>
醬油5大匙、酒1大匙、清水3杯、糖1大匙、太白粉水1茶匙

Ingredients
10 chicken wings
10 dried black mushrooms (small sized)
450g. bamboo shoot
1 stalk green onion
2 slices ginger
4 cups oil for deep fry
a few cilantro

seasonings
5 tbsp. soy sauce
1 tbsp. wine
3 cups boiling water
1 tbsp. sugar
1 tsp. cornstarch paste

Procedures
1. Cut off the sharp portion of the chicken wings. Place it into a bowl and mix with the soy sauce for about 10 minutes. Deep fry it until golden brown. Remove and drain.
2. Soak the dried black mushrooms with water until soft. Remove the stems. Cut the bamboo shoots into triangular shapes. Deep fry for 1/2 minute.
3. Heat 2 tbsp. oil. Stir fry the green onion and ginger until brown. Add the remaining soy sauce from soaking the chicken, then add wine, sugar and boiling water. Place the chicken wings in the middle row, mushrooms and bamboo shoots on the side. Cover and cook for 20 minutes until the sauce is reduced to 1 cup.
4. Add cornstarch paste and stir the sauce until it has thickened. Splash 1 tbsp. hot oil on top. Remove to the serving platter. Garnish with some cilantro. Serve.

做法 >>

1. 將雞翅膀每支由關節處分切成兩段,不用翅尖只用整支雞翅,放入大碗內加入醬油5大匙,醃約10分鐘,再投入燒熱之油中炸黃,撈出。
2. 冬菇泡軟,剪除菇蒂備用。冬筍切成對開4半的直條尖角塊狀,也用熱油炸半分鐘,撈出留用。
3. 用2大匙油爆香蔥、薑後倒下醃雞翅所餘之醬油,並淋下酒,再放糖及開水,然後將雞翅排放在鍋中央,而左右兩旁分別放下冬菇與冬筍,蓋上鍋蓋,以小火燒煮約20分鐘,至湯汁僅餘下1杯為止。
4. 將太白粉水緩緩由鍋邊淋下,並端起鍋子略做旋轉式搖動,以使太白粉流散均勻,見略有黏度即可淋下熱油1大匙以增光亮,輕輕推至大盤內排列。上面飾放香菜少許以增美觀。

香酥雞
Flavored Crispy Chicken

材料 >>
嫩雞1隻（約1.5公斤重）、炸油8杯、醬油2大匙、麵粉3大匙、花椒鹽2茶匙

醃雞料 >>
花椒2大匙、鹽2大匙、蔥3支、酒1大匙

做法 >>

1. 將雞先用力壓扁。在乾的炒鍋內用小火炒香花椒粒。再放下鹽略為拌炒，盛入盤中，再放下拍碎的蔥段及酒拌合，用來擦搓雞之全身內外，約搓2分鐘後放置在盆中醃上4至8小時。

2. 將醃過之雞放在盤上，移進蒸鍋內，（將醃雞之各材料放入雞肚中），用大火蒸2小時以上至雞十分酥爛為止，由蒸籠中端出，將肚中之蔥等取出。

3. 用醬油塗抹雞身四周，並撒下乾麵粉拍勻，投入熱油中，用大火炸兩次至雞身呈金黃色即好。

4. 將雞胸部向上放在大盤中間，四周圍放荷葉夾或麵包片，並備花椒鹽在盤邊，上桌供食。（將雞肉夾放在荷葉夾內食之）

Ingredients
1 whole chicken (about 1.5Kg.)
8 cups oil for deep fry
2 tbsp. soy sauce
3 tbsp. flour
2 tsp. brown pepper corn salt

To marinate chicken
2 tbsp. brown pepper corn
2 tbsp. salt
3 green onions
1 tbsp. wine

Procedures

1. Set a Chinese wok or frying pan over low heat. Stir fry brown pepper corns until fragrant, add salt, stir fry until the salt turn to yellowish. Remove to a large bowl and let cool. Mix with green onion (crush and cut into 1" long) and wine.

2. Clean and wipe the chicken. Rub the inside and outside with No. 1. Let it stary for 4 to 8 hours.

3. Place the chicken in a bowl. Steam over high heat for at least 2 hours until very tender.

4. Remove the chicken, wipe it dry. Brush soy sauce all over the chicken. Powder with flour. Deep fry in heated oil over high heat until brown and crispy. (It is better to fry twice).

5. Put the fried chicken on a platter (breast side up). Serve with brown pepper corn salt and steamed flower-shape buns. (sliced bread or egg roll wrappers may be substituted). Separate the chicken with chop sticks and place chicken meat inside the bun.

花椒鹽之做法，係將花椒粒1大匙用小火炒香後加入鹽2大匙再略炒一下，再全部研磨成粉末便是。(可一次多做一些放在瓶中備用》

Brown pepper corn salt is made with 1 tbsp. brown pepper corn and 2 tbsp. salt. Stir over low heat in a dried frying pan for about 1 minute. When the salt is brown and fragrant, let it cool. Then grind it finely. Sift with a very fine sieve. Keep it in a tightly covered bottle. Most of the Chinese deep fried dishes use it as a dipping sauce.

石榴雞
Pomegranate Shaped Chicken

註 此菜也可將材料生拌之後包入,而炸的時間要長久些,也頗鮮嫩可口。由於形狀似石榴故而得名。

This dish is also delicious if one uses all uncooked ingredients to wrap in the paper. Deep fry over low heat for 3 minutes until it is done.

材料 >>
雞肉250公克、洋蔥丁1/2杯、青椒丁1/2杯、荸薺6個、香菇2朵、芹菜屑2大匙、胡蘿蔔片20小片、玻璃紙(5"×15")12張、細青蒜葉(或韭菜葉)12支、炸油6杯

醃雞料 >>
蛋白1大匙、太白粉1大匙、醬油2茶匙、糖1/3茶匙

綜合調味料 >>
酒1/2大匙、醬油1大匙、糖1茶匙、鹽1/4茶匙、醋1茶匙、太白粉1茶匙、胡椒粉1/4茶匙、麻油1/2茶匙

做法 >>

1. 將雞肉先輕輕剁數下後，連皮切成1公分大小之四方丁，全部用醃雞料拌勻，醃約半小時。
2. 荸薺與泡軟的香菇均切成小碎片（如指甲片大小）。
3. 將1杯油燒熱後傾下雞丁，過油炒約10秒鐘即行撈出瀝乾（雞丁應保持半熟狀）。
4. 用2大匙油炒一下洋蔥（約10秒鐘）隨即放下香菇、青椒、荸薺、胡蘿蔔片及雞丁，並將綜合調味料倒下，大火炒拌均勻，熄火後將芹菜屑落鍋再拌勻即盛出。
5. 用玻璃紙分別包住約1大匙半的雞丁料，使成為圓球體之石榴形狀，四周之玻璃紙收緊在頂上後用燙熟之青蒜絲或韭菜葉綁好，做成石榴狀。
6. 將炸油燒至八分熱後，放進石榴雞，小火炸約1分半鐘。瀝乾油後排列在大盤內上桌。

Ingredients

250g. chicken meat
1/2 cup diced onion
1/2 cup diced green pepper
6 water chestnuts
2 black mushrooms
2 tbsp. diced celery
20 slices carrot (cooked)
12 pieces cellophane paper (5" × 15")
12 thin spring onions or leeks
6 cup oil for deep fry

To marinate chicken

1 tbsp. egg while
1 tbsp. cornstarch
2 tsp. soy sauce
1/3 tsp. sugar

seasonings

1/2 tbsp. wine
1 tbsp. soy sauce
1 tsp. sugar
1/4 tsp. salt
1 tsp. vinegar
1 tsp. cornstarch
1/4 tsp. black pepper
1/2 tsp. sesame oil

Procedures

1. After pounding the chicken meat with the cleaver, cut it into 1cm squares. Marinate for about 1/2 hour.
2. Cut the soaked mushrooms and water chestnuts into small slices.
3. Heat 1 cup of oil in a pan, stir fry the chicken for about 10 seconds until the chicken looks half done. Remove the chicken.
4. Use another 2 tbsp. oil to stir fry the onion for about 10 seconds, add all vegetables (except celery), chicken, and seasonings. Stir until evenly. Turn off the heat and add the celery, mix again.
5. Place 1 1/2 tbsp. the chicken mixture in the center of a paper. Fold all of the edges to top center. The chicken package should be round with a swirl design on top. Wrap it with boiled spring onion or leeks string tightly.
6. Deep fry the chicken package in about 160°C hot oil for about 1 1/2 minute over low heat. Remove and drain the oil. Place attractively on a platter, serve.

紅燒八寶雞
Stuffed Chicken with Treasures

材料 >>
全雞1隻（約1.5公斤重）、蔥屑1大匙、香菇丁1/3杯、火腿丁1/3杯、蝦米丁1/4杯、筍丁（或蓮子）1/2杯、雞肫1個（切丁）、糯米飯2 1/2杯、醬油2大匙、炸油6杯

調味料 >>
酒1大匙、醬油1大匙、鹽1/2茶匙

燒雞用料 >>
蔥3支、薑2片、八角1顆、酒1大匙、醬油4大匙、碎冰糖1/2大匙、開水4杯

Ingredients

1 chicken about 1.5 Kg., 1 tbsp. chopped green onion, 1/3 cup diced mushrooms, 1/3 cup diced ham, 1/4 cup chopped dry shrimp, 1/2 cup diced bamboo shoot (or lotus seeds), 1 chicken gizzard (diced), 2 1/2 cups cooked glutinous rice, 2 tbsp. soy sauce (to rub the chicken), 6 cups oil for deep fry

Seasonings

(A) 1 tbsp. wine, 1 tbsp. soy sauce, 1/2 tsp. salt
(B) 3 stalks green onion, 2 slices ginger, 1 star anise, 1 tbsp. soy sauce, 1/2 tbsp. sugar, 4 cups boiling water

Procedures

1 Use kitchen scissors or a sharp knife to cut the membranes around the chicken neck. Stretch it and remove all the bones from the chicken, without changing its original shape.
2 Heat 2 tbsp. oil to stir fry the green onion, mushrooms, ham, dry shrimp, bamboo shoot, and the diced chicken gizzard. Sprinkle wine and soy sauce when fragrant, season with salt. Stir fry constantly. Turn off the heat. Add the glutinous rice and mix thoroughly (this is the stuffing).
3 Stuff the glutinous rice mixture into the cavity of the chicken and seal the tail opening with a needle and thread or tooth picks. Rub all over the chicken skin with 2 tbsp. of soy sauce.
4 Deep fry the stuffed chicken over high heat until golden brown. Drain off the oil.
5 Cut the green onions into long sections, arrange it on the bottom of a pan. Put the chicken on top and add the seasonings (B) in. Cook over medium low heat for about 1 1/2 hours until the sauce is reduced to 2/3 cup.
6 Remove the chicken to a serving platter. Thicken the sauce with cornstarch paste. Splash this sauce over the chicken. Serve.

做法 >>

1 將雞由脖頸處割開雞皮，連雞肉一起慢慢用刀切割剝下，使雞之大骨可以剔下（即半拆）而雞仍保持原形狀。
2 燒熱油2大匙，爆香蔥屑，放下香菇、火腿、蝦米、筍和雞肫等同炒，淋酒及醬油，加鹽調味，熄火後放下糯米飯，仔細拌勻。
3 將上項材料塞入雞肚內（不可裝太滿），收口處用針線縫合好，雞皮上用手指塗抹2大匙醬油著色。
4 將炸油在鍋內燒熱，放下八寶雞炸黃，撈出瀝乾，將炸油倒出。
5 將蔥切成長段鋪在鍋底，再把雞放在上面，再將其他燒雞用料全部加入鍋中，用中小火燒煮1 1/2小時，至湯汁僅餘2/3杯時止。
6 將雞小心盛到大盤內（先拆除縫口處之線），鍋中之湯汁用少許太白粉水勾芡後即淋到雞身上，並在上面綴以香菜即可上桌供食。

雞肉篇
培梅食譜II

辣子雞丁
Diced Chicken with Peppers

醃雞料 >>
蛋白1大匙、醬油1大匙、太白粉1大匙、水1大匙

綜合調味料 >>
淡色醬油2大匙、醋1大匙、糖1/2茶匙、鹽1/4茶匙、太白粉1茶匙、麻油少許、胡椒粉少許

材料 >>
嫩雞半隻（約1公斤）（或雞肉450公克）、大青椒1個、紅辣椒3支、蔥2支、薑15小片、油2杯

Ingredients
450g. chicken meat
1 green pepper
3 hot red peppers
2 stalks green onion
15 slices ginger (1/2" × 1/2"),
2 cups oil

To marinate chicken
1 tbsp. egg white
1 tbsp. soy sauce
1 tbsp. cornstarch
1 tbsp. water

seasoning sauce
2 tbsp. light colored soy sauce
1 tbsp. brown vinegar
1/2 tsp. sugar
1/4 tsp. salt
1 tsp. cornstarch
1/4 tsp. sesame oil
1/4 tsp. black pepper

Procedures
1. Cut the chicken into 1.5cm cubes. Marinate with mixed marinades for at least 30 minutes.
2. Dice the green pepper, red peppers, and green onion.
3. In a small bowl, mix the seasoning sauce thoroughly.
4. Heat the oil to 160°C. Fry the diced chicken for about 15 seconds. Remove and drain off the oil from frying pan.
5. Heat another 2 tbsp. oil to stir fry the green onion, ginger, green pepper and red pepper for about 10 seconds, add the chicken and the seasoning sauce. Stir over high heat until the sauce is thickened and mixed thoroughly. Transfer to a platter and serve hot.

 此菜如喜食辣味，可在綜合調味料內加入辣椒醬若干。
If you like really spicy things, you may add some hot chili paste or Tabasco sauce to the seasoning sauce.

做法 >>

1. 將雞骨除淨，約可得450公克雞肉，先把所有帶筋及肉厚的部份，用刀輕輕拍鬆，連皮切成1.5公分四方大小之丁狀，盛入大碗中用醃雞肉料拌勻，醃約半小時以上。
2. 青、紅辣洗淨去籽後，切成與雞肉同樣大小之方塊；蔥切1.5公分長斜段；薑切小片備用。
3. 用一只小碗將綜合調味料準備好。
4. 將油燒成8分熱後，倒下醃過之雞丁，泡炸15秒鐘至雞丁轉白即可撈出，餘油倒出。
5. 另在鍋內燒熱2大匙油後，爆炒蔥段、薑片及青、紅辣椒丁，翻炒數下後即倒下雞丁，同時淋下綜合調味料，用大火迅速拌炒均勻，熄火即盛出。

雞凍
Jellied Chicken

材料 >>
雞半隻（約1公斤）、豬肉皮150公克、蔥2支、薑3片、八角1顆、香菜少許

調味料 >>
醬油4大匙、酒1大匙、糖1/2大匙、鹽1/2茶匙

做法 >>
1. 雞洗淨，連骨斬剁成小塊（約2.5公分之四方塊）。豬肉皮刮淨皮上之污穢後切成5公分大小，同雞肉一起用開水燙1分鐘，撈出、洗淨。
2. 將肉皮和雞塊放入鍋中，加入滾水5杯及蔥、薑、八角和其他調味料，先用大火燒滾後，即改為小火，慢燉30分鐘左右。
3. 將雞塊先撈出，再將豬皮也撈出放在砧板上，用刀剁成碎屑，再重放回鍋內用小火燒約10分鐘，使汁黏稠而只剩1 1/2杯左右。
4. 將鍋內之湯汁過濾一下，然後將雞肉重行落鍋，續用小火煮3分鐘左右，即可全部倒入大碗內，待其冷透後移進冰箱中。
5. 食時可倒扣在盤中或用筷子分成小塊，裝入碟內。

Ingredients
1/2 chicken (about 1Kg.), 150g. pork rind (or 2 packs of unflavored gelatin), 2 stalks green onion, 3 slices ginger, 1 star anise

Seasonings
4 tbsp. soy sauce, 1 tbsp. wine, 1/2 tbsp. sugar, 1/2 tsp. salt

Procedures
1. Cut the chicken with bones into pieces (about 2.5cm big). Cut the pork rind into 5cm large pieces. Boil all in boiling water only for one minute. Remove and discard the water.
2. Place the chicken and the pork rind into a pan. Add 5 cups of boiling water, green onions, ginger, star anise, and all seasonings. Bring to a boil. Reduce the heat to low. Cook for about half an hour until the juice is reduced to 1 1/2 cups.
3. Remove the chicken to a bowl. Chop the pork rind into very small pieces. Put it back into the pan, and cook for another 10 minutes over low heat until the broth is rather thick.
4. Filter the broth and put the chicken back to pan. Cook for 3 more minutes over low heat. Pour all into a bowl. When it has cooled to room temperature, place it in the refrigerator until it is firm enough. (it will take more than 1 hour).
5. Turn the bowl upside down on a plate and remove the bowl or separate the jellied chicken with chopsticks and put it on a plate. Serve cold.

此係北方雞凍的做法，同樣方法可參照做蹄花凍，小排骨凍或雞翅膀凍等。
Pig's feet, chicken wings, or spareribs can be used instead of chicken.

生炒雞鬆
Stir-fried Minced Chicken

材料 >>
雞肉250公克、香菇丁1/2杯、洋火腿丁1/2杯、筍丁1/2杯、韭黃丁1杯、蠶豆瓣或青豆1/2杯、蛋2個、油1杯、米粉50公克、薄餅12張

拌雞肉料 >>
鹽1/4茶匙、太白粉2茶匙、水1大匙

綜合調味料 >>
鹽1/2茶匙、淡色醬油1 1/2大匙、太白粉1茶匙、麻油1茶匙、清湯2大匙、胡椒粉少許

註 薄餅（又名單餅）做法在培梅食譜第一冊318頁。
The recipe for "dan-bing", a thin Chinese pancake, can be found on page 318 of "Pei Mei's Chinese Cook Book Vol. I".

做法 >>
1. 將米粉用燒得極熱之油炸泡,至成金黃色酥脆為止(每面各炸3秒鐘)。撈出後瀝乾,置大盤中壓碎,堆成小山形。
2. 雞肉切成小丁(如綠豆粒大小),全部用拌料拌好,放置片刻之後,用1杯溫油炒熟,瀝出備用。
3. 將蛋打散,煎成蛋皮,然後切成0.6公分大小之丁狀備用。
4. 另燒熱2大匙油炒香菇丁、筍丁、蠶豆瓣及洋火腿丁等,約1分鐘後,傾入雞丁與蛋皮丁,再淋下綜合調味料,用大火拌炒均勻,最後將韭黃丁撒下即熄火,略加拌鏟即可盛在炸米粉上。
5. 在另外小碟中盛放做好之薄餅或春捲皮一起上桌,食時在薄餅中放雞鬆1大匙多,包捲而食。

Ingredients

250g. chicken breast
1/2 cup diced mushrooms (or soaked black mushrooms)
1/2 cup diced ham
1 cup diced bamboo shoot
1 cup of diced white Leeks
1/2 cup green beans (cooked)
2 eggs
1 cup oil
50g. rice noodles
12 pieces dan-bing (or egg roll wrappers)

To marinate chicken

1/4 tsp. salt
2 tsp. cornstarch
1 tbsp. cold water

Seasoning sauce

1/2 tsp. salt
1 1/2 tbsp. light colored soy sauce
1 tsp. cornstarch
1 tsp. sesame oil
2 tbsp. soup stock
1/8 tsp. black pepper

Procedures

1. Heat oil until very hot. Deep fry the rice noodles until puffed and light browned (only 2 or 3 seconds for each side). Remove and put on a platter. Crush them with a fork or chopsticks.
2. Cut the chicken into very small cubes. Marinate for 10 minutes. Then stir-fry with 1 cup of hot oil only for 30 seconds and drain.
3. Make a thin pancake with the beaten eggs. Cut into 0.6cm cubes.
4. Heat 2 tbsp. oil in a pan. Stir-fry mushrooms, bamboo shoot, green beans, and ham. After 1 minute, add chicken, egg cubes, and seasoning sauce. Stir fry over high heat until mixture thickens. Add the white leeks at last. Turn off the heat right away. Place on the platter over fried rice noodles.
5. Serve with dan-bing or egg roll wrapper which will be used to wrap around the meat and rice noodle mixture.

雀巢雞丁
Stir-fried Chicken in Bird's Nest

材料 >>
雞胸肉450公克、草菇10個、青椒丁1杯、荸薺（或筍丁）1/2杯、胡蘿蔔花片（煮熟）20小片、蔥小丁3大匙、薑小片1大匙、馬鈴薯450公克、太白粉1杯、鹽1/3茶匙、炸油8杯

醃雞料 >>
蛋白1大匙、太白粉1 1/2大匙、醬油1大匙

Ingredients
450g. chicken meat, 10 mushrooms (cut into slices), 1 cup diced green peppers (1/2" cube), 1/2 cup sliced water chestnuts (or diced bamboo shoot), 20 slices cooked carrot, 3 tbsp. diced green onion, 1 tbsp. sliced ginger, 450g. potatoes, 1/3 tsp. salt, 1 cup cornstarch, 8 cups oil for deep fry

To marinate chicken
1 tbsp. egg white, 1 1/2 tbsp. cornstarch, 1 tbsp. light colored soy sauce

Seasoning sauce
2 tbsp. light colored soy sauce, 1/2 tbsp. cornstarch, 1 tbsp. wine, 1/4 tsp. salt, 1/2 tsp. sugar, 2 tbsp. water, 1/4 tsp. black pepper, 1/2 tsp. sesame oil

Procedures
1. Dice the chicken into 2cm pieces and marinate for 1/2 hour. Fry in 2 cups of oil (about 160ºC) until the meat becomes white and then drain.
2. Heat the pan with 3 tbsp. of oil and stir-fry green onion, ginger, mushrooms, water chestnuts, carrot, and green pepper. Then add the chicken cubes and the seasoning sauce. Turn to high heat. Stir evenly and pour all into the bird's' nest.
3. Bird's nest: Cut the potatoes into thin shreds. Rinse with cold water, drain it dry. Place into a bowl and mix with 1/3 tsp. salt and 1 cup cornstarch. Then place potato shreds in one strainer and press upon it with another strainer, deep fry both in very hot oil for about 4 minutes until golden brown. Drain and take the bird's nest out from the strainer
4. Shred and deep fry some green vegetables or shred some lettuce, place under the nest for decoration.

綜合調味料 >>

醬油2大匙、太白粉1/2大匙、酒1大匙、鹽1/4茶匙、糖1/2茶匙、水2大匙、胡椒1/4茶匙、麻油1/2茶匙

做法 >>

1. 雞肉切成2公分四方大之小丁後,用醃雞料醃約半小時。用燒至八分熱的炸油2杯泡炸至熟,撈出瀝乾。
2. 起油鍋用約3大匙油大火爆炒蔥、薑,並加入草菇片、青椒丁、荸薺丁、胡蘿蔔片等同炒,然後將雞丁合入,並淋下綜合調味料(需預先準備妥在一小碗內),用大火急加炒拌均勻。裝入雀巢中。
3. 雀巢之做法:將馬鈴薯切成細絲後,用冷水沖過並瀝乾水份,放在大碗內,加鹽及太白粉同拌,在一只漏勺內鋪滿馬鈴薯絲,再用另一只漏勺在上面壓住,輕輕放進熱油中炸約4分鐘,至成為金黃色而已酥脆為止,瀝乾油後輕輕取下馬鈴薯,即為雀巢。
4. 將炸過之芥蘭菜葉絲或生的生菜絲鋪在雀巢下,以增美觀。

鴨肉篇

鴨各部份之用途

鴨在中國菜中常被列為主菜之一種，通常多用整隻鴨烹調，也可將一隻分為2～3種吃法，例如：去骨八寶鴨，只採用鴨皮及部分鴨肉，其餘鴨肉則可切片或切絲，再酌加一些配料，或炒、或扒、或拌、或溜，也可取最嫩部份做「湯泡鴨脯」（湖南名菜），鴨骨加蔬菜、豆腐、粉絲等燉湯，實為營養可口之大鍋菜。

燴鴨掌與鴨舌本屬京菜中之名餚，但限於原料收購之不易，家常已很少烹製。又鴨腎（肫）、鴨肝等可炒食，也可酥炸、軟煎及做什錦菜餡之配料，用處頗為廣泛。另外鴨肫和肝又可與鴨翅膀等一些燒滷，成為冷盤或零食之一味。

About Duck

Duck is considered to be one of the most important Chinese dishes. Usually, a whole duck is used, but one duck can be used for three completely different dishes. For example:

1. "Eight treasures Duck" uses the duck's skin and some meat.
2. Some of the other meat can be sliced or and used to stir fry, fraised, or as a salad with other ingredients. The most tender meat can be used to make "Duck Breast soup." (a famous Hunan dish).
3. The duck bones can be stewed with vegetables and bean curd to make a very nutritious soup. The duck's webbed feet and tongue are used to make famous Beijing dishes, but since the accompanying ingredients are not easy to buy, they are seldom served at home. The gizzard and liver can be stir fried, deep fried, or used as accompanying ingredients in many dishes. Another common way of cooking the duck's gizzard, liver, and wings is to boil them in spicy brown sauce and serve them as a cold dish.

Some American ducks are much fatter and greasier than Chinese. roasting chicken would work well in duck recipes if Chinese duck or Long Island duck is not available.

鹽水鴨

Spiced Duck Cold Cuts

材料 >>
光鴨1隻（約1.8公斤重）

醃鴨料 >>
花椒2大匙、鹽2 1/2大匙、硝1茶匙（可免）

煮鴨料 >>
水10杯、鹽2大匙、糖1大匙、酒4大匙、桂皮（2.5公分長）2片、八角4顆、小茴1大匙、薑3大片、蔥5支

做法 >>
1. 買一隻無頭無內臟之光鴨，挖出腹內之鴨油後，洗淨，拭乾水份。
2. 將花椒在鍋內乾炒半分鐘，再加入鹽繼續炒到鹽轉為黃色，裝入大盆後加入硝（磨成粉狀）拌勻，用手抓起此醃鴨料在鴨身內外抹擦（應用力多擦數遍），放置6小時以上（不可超過2天）。
3. 燒一鍋開水，將鴨放入燙一下，待水再沸滾時，將鴨撈出，用冷水洗淨。
4. 在鍋內將煮鴨料燒滾（五香料需預先包紮好），然後將鴨放進鍋內（鴨腹向下放進），用很小火候煮上40分鐘左右。（中途需翻一次身）熄火。
5. 將鴨浸泡在鍋中至湯冷後，把鴨提出，放在盤上，待水份收乾後才可連骨斬切成1公分寬，5公分長之條狀或片狀小塊，整齊的排列在碟中供食。

Ingredients
1 whole duck (about 1.8 kg.)

Marinades
2 tbsp. brown pepper corn
2 1/2 tbsp. salt
1 tbsp. saltpeter

To cook the duck
10 cups cold water
2 tbsp. salt
1 tbsp. sugar
4 tbsp. wine
2 pieces (2.5cm long) cinnamon sticks
4 star anise
3 slices ginger
5 stalks green onion

Procedures
1. Rinse the duck. Then pat it dry with a paper towel.
2. Stir fry the brown pepper corn over low heat in a dry frying pan for 1/2 minute and then add salt and stir until the salt turns light browned. Place into a large bowl. Add the saltpepter and mix thoroughly. Rub both the out side and the inside of the duck with the salt mixture. Let the duck stand for at least 6 hours (don't marinate it over 2 days).
3. Boil the duck in a pot of boiling water. When the water boils again, remove the duck from the pot. Rinse it again.
4. Boil 10 cups of water. Add the seasonings to cook the duck (the spices should be wrapped in a bag). Place the duck into the pan (breast side down). Cover and cook for about 40 minutes over very low heat, (turn it over once after 20 minutes). Turn off the heat. Remove the duck after the broth becomes cold.
5. Chop the duck with the bones into 1cm wide, and 5cm long pieces. Arrange on a platter and serve cold.

鴨肉篇
培梅食譜II

鍋燒鴨
Fried Duck Pan Cake

材料 >>
鴨半隻（約1.2公斤重）、豬肉100公克、筍絲2/3杯、冬菇絲1/3杯、蔥絲2大匙、薑絲1/2大匙

調味料 >>
鹽1茶匙、胡椒粉少許

蛋麵糊料 >>
蛋3個、麵粉6大匙、太白粉3大匙、清水1大匙

沾鴨料 >>
糖3大匙、蕃茄醬2大匙、鎮江醋1大匙、鹽1/3茶匙、太白粉1茶匙、麻油少許、水4大匙、蔥屑1大匙

做法 >>
1. 將鴨與豬肉均用開水煮熟（約30分鐘）。待涼後去骨，切成3～4公分長之粗絲。
2. 在另一只碗內將蛋打散，調好蛋麵糊。
3. 將鴨肉、豬肉、冬菇、筍、蔥、薑各絲同置大碗中，加鹽和胡椒調味，拌勻再加入上項之蛋麵糊仔細拌合均勻。
4. 在炒鍋內燒1大匙油，炒香沾鴨料，撒下蔥屑便分裝在兩只小碗內。
5. 將平底煎鍋燒至極熱，放入多量的油（約2/3杯），待油熱時，即將第3項之材料全部倒下，用鏟子按壓攤平（使成餅狀），用小火反覆煎黃兩面至完全熟透為止（大約10分鐘）。
6. 取出後切成尖角小塊，全部排列在餐盤中，與沾汁同時上桌。

Ingredients
1/2 duck (about 1.2kg.), 100g. pork (shoulder), 2/3 cup shredded bamboo shoots, 1/3 cup shredded mushrooms, 2 tbsp. shredded green onion, 1/2 tbsp. shredded ginger

Seasonings
1 tsp. salt, 1/6 tsp. black pepper

Flour Batter
3 eggs, 6 tbsp. flour, 3 tbsp. cornstarch, 1 tbsp. cold water

Dipping sauce
3 tbsp. sugar, 2 tbsp. ketchup, 1 tbsp. vinegar, 1/3 tsp. salt, 1 tsp. cornstarch, 1/4 tsp. sesame oil, 4 tbsp. cold water, 1 tbsp. chopped green onion

Procedures
1. Cook the duck and pork in boiling water until done (about 30 minutes). Remove and let it cools, remove the bones from duck then cut both into strings about 3~4cm long.
2. In a large bowl, prepare the flour batter.
3. Add the duck, pork, mushrooms, bamboo shoot, green onion and ginger to the flour batter. Then season it with salt and pepper. Mix well.
4. Heat 1 tbsp. oil in a frying pan, add dipping sauce, bring it to a boil. Remove to two small bowls.
5. Heat 2/3 cup of oil. Pour the duck mixture in. Flatten and press with a spatula to from a round pan cake shape. Fry for 5 minutes over low heat. Turn it over and fry for another 5 minutes, until both sides turn golden brown and completely done.
6. Remove and cut it into small diagonal pieces. Arrange on a platter. Serve with the dipping sauce.

涼拌鴨條
Roast Duck Salad

材料 >>
熟鴨肉（燒鴨、滷鴨或白煮鴨皆可）250公克、芹菜 200公克、鹽1茶匙、綠豆芽1 1/2杯、芥末粉1/2 大匙、清水2大匙

綜合調味料 >>
芝麻醬1大匙、淡色醬油1 1/2大匙、清湯1大匙、糖1/2茶匙、鹽1/3茶匙、麻油1茶匙、白芝麻（炒香並壓碎）1/2大匙

做法 >>
1. 將鴨肉切成4公分長、與筷子相同粗細之條狀，整齊的排列在碟子中。
2. 芹菜摘除根與葉子後，在6杯燒滾之開水中燙煮10秒鐘（水中先加入鹽1茶匙）撈出後沖過冷開水，並擠乾，放在砧板上，整束切成4公分長段，也排在碟中。
3. 另將綠豆芽用開水燙5秒鐘，撈出後沖過冷開水，擠乾，堆放在碟子中。
4. 將芥末粉盛在小碗內，加清水調勻成稀糊狀，放在溫暖處（如有熱度之電鍋或蒸鍋上）3分鐘之後，見芥末糊已有辣味時便取出。
5. 用另一小碗調備綜合調味料（先把芝麻醬加醬油攪拌均勻，再將其他調味料加入）與芥末糊及鴨條同時上桌，食時淋下，略加拌合即可。（也可分別沾食）

Ingredients
250g. duck meat (cooked or roasted), 200g. celery, 1 tsp. salt, 1 1/2 cups bean sprouts, 1/2 tbsp. mustard powder (make paste), 2 tbsp. cold water (make paste)

Seasoning sauce
1 tbsp. sesame paste, 1 1/2 tbsp. light colored soy sauce, 1 tbsp. soup stock, 1/2 tsp. sugar, 1/3 tsp. salt, 1 tsp. sesame oil, 1/2 tbsp. roasted sesame seeds

Procedures
1. Cut the duck into 0.7cm wide, 4cm long stripes. Arrange on a plate.
2. Trim the celery, boil it in boiling water for 10 seconds. Remove and plunge into cold water. Squeeze dry. Cut into 4cm long stripes. Place on the plate.
3. Blanch the bean sprouts in boiling water for about 5 seconds. Remove and rinse it, then squeeze it dry, place on the plate.
4. Mix the mustard powder with cold water in a bowl. Keep in a warm place for 3 minutes until the mustard gets hot.
5. In another small bowl, combine all the seasoning sauce. Serve the duck salad with seasoning sauce and mustard sauce. Before eating, pour the sauce over the salad, mix it thoroughly. (You may dip the duck or vegetables into the seasoning sauce and mustard).

汽鍋鴨塊
Steamed Duck in Yunnan Casserole

材料 >>

光鴨半隻（約1公斤重）、瘦中國火腿100公克、薑8小片、開水3杯

調味料 >>

酒2大匙、鹽1茶匙

做法 >>

1. 將鴨連骨剁成2.5公分寬，4～5公分長之塊狀，放入滾水中燙1分鐘，撈出後用冷水沖洗一下，瀝乾水份。
2. 將鴨塊放進汽鍋中，並放下切成小丁塊的火腿，薑片也撒在上面。
3. 將開水倒進汽鍋中，加入鹽和酒，蓋上汽鍋之鍋蓋，再將汽鍋放進一個大鍋中，（大鍋之底部應舖墊一塊毛巾），注入冷水到大鍋內（水量不可超過汽鍋之把柄處），用小火燉蒸汽鍋3小時，大鍋中水不夠時應加入滾水續蒸，蒸至鴨肉十分酥爛為止，再加適量鹽調味。
4. 將汽鍋端上飯桌即可分食，湯清而味美，鴨肉香爛可口。

Ingredients
1/2 duck (about 1 kg.)
100g. Chinese ham
8 slices ginger
3 cups boiling water

Seasoning sauce
2 tbsp. wine
1 tsp. salt

Procedures
1. Cut the duck with bones into 2.5cm wide, 4~5cm long pieces. Boil duck for about 1 minute in boiling water. Remove and rinse with cold water. Drain it dry.
2. Place the duck into the special style of casserole (Yunnan style). Add the diced Chinese ham and ginger.
3. Add the boiling water, wine, and salt into the casserole. Cover it. Place the casserole into a large pot. (on the bottom of the large pot, put a towel under casserole). Add cold water to the large pot until it covers half of the handle of the casserole. Covered and cook for about 3 hours until the duck is tender. Add more hot water while cook, if necessary.
4. Remove the casserole from the large pot. Season with some salt, if needed. Serve hot.

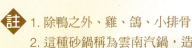 1. 除鴨之外、雞、鴿、小排骨、牛肉、牛尾、鰻魚等也可用汽鍋蒸煮。
2. 這種砂鍋稱為雲南汽鍋,造型特殊,利用中間的汽孔將蒸汽導入鍋中,故湯汁清而鮮美。沒有汽鍋時可以用燉盅來蒸,湯汁亦很清爽。

1. Instead of duck, chicken, pigeon, beef, pork ribs, ox-tail or eel may be used.
2. This kind of casserole is a special shaped casserole. In the middle of the bottom at the casserole is a chimney. When the water boils, the steam rises through the chimney to the duck. Since there is only a little soup, the duck maintains its original flavor. In Chinese, this kind of casserole is called "steam casserole". You may use a bowl to steam the duck, if you don't have a steam casserole.

芋泥鴨

Mashed Taro on Crispy Duck

材料 >>
鴨半隻（約1公斤重）、大芋頭（或洋芋）450公克、澄麵（或太白粉）2/3杯、蝦米（切小丁）1大匙、臘肉丁（或香腸、火腿丁）2大匙、太白粉2大匙、生菜葉（切絲）1杯、炸油8杯

蒸鴨料 >>
醬油2大匙、八角1顆、蔥1支、薑2片、花椒1茶匙

芋頭調味料 >>
豬油3大匙、胡椒粉1/4茶匙、鹽1/3茶匙

沾汁料 >>
糖1/2茶匙、鹽1/4茶匙、太白粉1茶匙、蠔油1大匙、清湯2/3杯、蔥屑2大匙

做法 >>

1. 將鴨抹乾皮上水份後，用蒸鴨料之醬油塗色並醃15分鐘，然後用燒得極熱之油，鴨皮向下，炸至皮呈褐黃色，撈出後放在碟子上（皮向上），將其餘的蒸鴨料散放在上面，並淋上醬油，置入鍋中，以大火蒸爛。（約1個半小時）

2. 將澄粉（或太白粉）放在盆內，淋下開水約1/3杯，燙成半熟狀，再揉合成一糰。

3. 在蒸鴨時一起把大芋頭（削皮切成大片）也蒸熟，取出趁熱用刀面壓碎成泥狀，並拌入豬油、燙過之澄粉、鹽、胡椒粉及蝦米丁、臘肉丁等，用手搓勻。

4. 將第一項蒸爛之鴨放冷之後，拆除全部骨頭（但不可弄碎），皮部向下放在撒了乾太白粉之盤內，鋪平鴨肉，再撒下太白粉少許，再將第3項之芋泥鋪在上面，並撒些乾太白粉，慢慢推到熱油中去炸（小火），炸至全部呈金黃色為止（約3分鐘），撈出、瀝乾。

5. 趁熱將炸好之芋泥鴨切成3公分四方小塊（或尖角塊也可）排列到菜盤上，盤底可鋪放切絲之生菜。上桌時另用兩只小碗裝沾汁同上，以供蘸用。

6. 味汁之做法：將所有沾汁材料用小火煮滾，放下蔥屑調勻即可。

Ingredients
1/2 duck (about 1 kg.)
450g. taro (or potato)
2/3 cup cornstarch
1 tbsp. dried shrimp (soaked and chopped)
2 tbsp. Chinese ham or sausage (chopped)
2 tbsp. cornstarch
1 cup shredded lettuce

To steam duck
2 tbsp. dark colored soy sauce
1 star anise
1 green onion
2 slices ginger
1 tsp. brown pepper corn

Seasonings for taro
3 tbsp. lard (or shortening)
1/3 tsp. salt
1/4 tsp. pepper

Dipping sauce
1/2 tsp. sugar
1/4 tsp. salt
1 tsp. cornstarch
1 tsp. oyster sauce
2/3 cup of soup stock
2 tbsp. chopped green onion

Procedures
1. Clean and wipe dry the duck. Put on a plate with skin side up. Rub the duck with soy sauce. Let it stay for 15 minutes. Deep fry the duck until golden brown. Drain. Put the fried duck on a plate. Put the spices for steaming duck on top of the duck. Steam over high heat for about 1 1/2 hours.
2. Add boiling water to cornstarch. Mix thoroughly and make a dough. Set aside.
3. Cut the taro into thick slices. Steam until soft (about 20 minutes). Mash it very fine. Place the mashed taro into a large bowl. Add chopped dry shrimp, chopped ham, salt, pepper, cornstarch dough and lard. Knead them thoroughly.
4. Put the duck on a flat plate with skin side down. Remove the bones from the duck. Also remove the spices. Sprinkle the whole surface of the duck with cornstarch. Then cover with all of the No. 3 taro mixture. Sprinkle the top with cornstarch again. Flatten and smooth the top. Slip the whole duck into heated oil. Deep fry over low heat until the out side turns golden brown.
5. Remove the fried duck and cut it into small diamond shaped pieces. Place on top of the shredded lettuce leaves.
6. Boil the dipping sauce in a sauce pan over low heat. After turning off the heat, add the chopped green onion in. Pour the sauce into 2 small bowls, serve with duck.

糯米封鴨塊

Steamed Duck Pudding

材料 >>

光鴨半隻（約1.2公斤）、糯米飯4杯、火腿（切丁）3大匙（或香腸，臘肉也可）、香菇2大匙、蝦米（泡軟）2大匙、蓮子（或花生米）1/3杯、鴨肫1個

調味料 >>

(A) 糖1/2茶匙、鹽1/4茶匙、酒1大匙、醬油2大匙、胡椒粉少許

(B) 酒1/2大匙、醬油1大匙、鹽1/3茶匙

做法 >>

1. 洗淨鴨內部後放入蒸鍋內，大火蒸約1小時至熟，取出待涼，小心用手拆去所有鴨骨，然後連皮切成約2.5公分寬之長方塊。

2. 在一只大碗內（或小型盆中）排列全部鴨肉（皮向下貼著碗底），再在另一個小碗內調好調味料(A)，由大碗的邊緣淋下，並輕輕轉動大碗，使鴨肉能吸收味道。

3. 在炒鍋內燒熱2大匙油後，爆炒切成小丁之香菇、蝦米、火腿、鴨肫（剔除白皮）及泡軟之蓮子，加調味料調味，即將火熄去。將煮好的糯米飯倒下，仔細拌合均勻。

4. 將上項糯米飯盛在鴨肉碗中，並略加攤平，壓緊後蓋上一個碟子，用大火蒸40分鐘至1小時。

5. 取出後倒扣在一只大餐盤內，即可上桌分食。

Ingredients

1/2 duck (about 1.2kg.)
4 cups cooked glutinous rice
3 tbsp. diced ham
2 tbsp. diced black mushroom
2 tbsp. dried shrimp (soaked and diced)
1/3 cup soaked lotus seeds (optional)
1 duck gizzard (diced)

Seasonings

(A) 1/2 tsp. sugar, 1/4 tsp. salt, 1 tbsp. wine, 2 tsp. soy sauce, 1/4 tsp. black pepper

(B) 1/2 tbsp. wine, 1 tbsp. soy sauce, 1/3 tsp. salt

Procedures

1. Put the duck in a bowl. Steam it over high heat for about one hour. Remove the duck and let it cools. Remove all the bones carefully from the duck. Cut the boneless duck into 2.5cm wide, 5cm long pieces (with skin). Arrange the duck attractively in the bottom of a large bowl (with skin side down).
2. In another small bowl, mix seasonings (A). Pour it around the edges of the duck bowl. Then turn and tilt the bowl slowly until all the duck is covered.
3. Heat 2 tbsp. oil to stir fry ham, mushrooms, dried shrimp, duck gizzards, and lotus seeds for about 1 minute. Splash in the wine, season with soy sauce and salt. Turn off the heat. Add the cooked glutinous rice in and mix evenly.
4. Place all the mixed rice into the bowl to cover the duck. Flatten and cover the surface with a plate, steam the duck pudding for 1 hour.
5. Reverse the duck pudding to a serving plate. Serve hot.

滷鴨
Braised Duck

材料 >>
嫩鴨1隻（約1.8公斤重）、深色醬油3大匙、炸油8杯

滷鴨料 >>
水7杯、蔥3支、薑3大片、八角2顆、桂皮（約5公分長）1片、碎冰糖（或白糖）3大匙、鹽1/2茶匙、酒2大匙、醬油2/3杯、白糖2大匙

Ingredients
1 whole duck (about 1.8 kg)
3 tbsp. dark colored soy sauce
8 cups oil for deep fry

To braised duck
7 cups of water
3 stalks green onion
3 slices ginger
2 star anise
1 cinnamon stick (about 5cm long)
3 tbsp. rock sugar (or regular sugar)
1/2 tsp. salt
2 tbsp. wine
2/3 cup soy sauce
2 tbsp. sugar

Procedures
1. Rub all of the duck skin with 3 tbsp. soy sauce. After it dries, deep fry the duck over high heat until golden brown. Remove the duck and drain off the oil.
2. Place the whole duck into a pan (breast side down). Add water and all the spices and condiments except 2 tbsp. sugar to the pan. Cover the lid and bring to a boil. Reduce to low heat, braise for about 2 1/2 hours. (Turn the duck over twice during braising.)
3. Remove the duck when it is tender, but still retains its original shape, and the sauce has been reduced to 1 1/2 cups.
4. Add 2 tbsp. sugar to the pan, stew over low heat for about 5 minutes until it thickened.
5. Cut the duck into small pieces. Arrange on a plate. Pour the sauce over the duck. Serve cold.

 註 通常一隻滷鴨可分為2次或多次吃完，故鴨上所淋之汁一次不可淋得太多。
This is an appetizer. A whole duck cooked in this way can be served at several meals.

做法 >>

1. 用醬油把鴨皮全部抹勻，稍加吹乾之後，再塗抹一次。放進燒得極熱之油中炸黃。撈出、瀝乾。
2. 將鴨整隻放在鍋內（鴨背向上），注入清水7杯，並加入所有滷鴨用的辛香料及調味料（除了白糖2大匙之外），大火煮滾，然後改用小火燒煮2個半小時（中途需翻兩次面）。
3. 燒煮至鴨已夠爛，但仍舊十分完整，而鍋中之滷汁僅餘下一杯半時止，將鴨鏟出。
4. 加入白糖2大匙到鍋內滷汁中，再用極小火候燒煮，約5分鐘至汁黏稠為止，盛出在小碗內。
5. 將鴨分切成小塊裝盤，淋下上項滷汁便成。

薑爆鴨絲
Quick Stir-fried Duck Shreds with Ginger

材料 >>
熟鴨（燒鴨或滷鴨）1/2 隻（約 600 公克）、大蒜片 2 大匙、紅辣椒絲 2 大匙、嫩薑絲 3 大匙、筍絲（4 公分長）2/3 杯、胡蘿蔔絲（4 公分長）1/3 杯、芹菜絲（4 公分長）1/2 杯、油 4 大匙

調味料 >>
酒 1 大匙、淡色醬油 1 1/2 大匙、鹽 1/3 茶匙、糖 1/2 茶匙、醋 1/2 大匙、麻油 1/2 茶匙

Ingredients
1/2 cooked or roasted duck (about 600g.)
2 tbsp. sliced garlic
2 tbsp. shredded hot red pepper
3 tbsp. shredded young ginger
2/3 cup of shredded bamboo shoot
1/3 cup of shredded carrot
1/2 cup of celery
4 tbsp. oil

Seasonings
1 tbsp. wine
1 1/2 tbsp. light colored soy sauce
1/3 tsp. salt
1/2 tsp. sugar
1/2 tbsp. vinegar
1/2 tsp. sesame oil

Procedures
1. Remove all of the bones from the duck. Cut the meat intol 4cm long shreds.
2. Fry the sliced garlic with 3 tbsp. heated oil. Then add the red pepper, ginger, and the duck. Stir a few seconds. Add the bamboo shoot and carrot. Splash wine and soy sauce. Season with salt and sugar. Add celery, vinegar and sesame oil. Continue to stirring until heated.
3. Remove to a plate and serve. Also you may serve with dan-bing or egg roll wrapper to wrap the dish and eat.

 1. 如無燒鴨或滷鴨，也可將生鴨用水煮熟，冷後使用（即熟鴨）。
2. 如無筍絲也可用綠豆芽代替。
3. 薄餅（即單餅）之做法可參照培梅食譜第一冊318頁。

1. You may roast a duck or make a braised soy sauce duck or just boil a duck to make this dish.
2. You may use bean sprouts instead of bamboo shoots.
3. The recipe for "dan-bing" can be found on page 318 of Pei Mei's Cook Book Vol. I.

做法 >>

1. 將鴨骨剔除,取全部鴨肉,連皮切成約4公分長之粗絲。
2. 在炒鍋內燒熱3大匙油後,先炒香大蒜片與紅辣椒絲,續將鴨絲、薑絲、筍絲及胡蘿蔔絲等落鍋用大火拌炒,淋下酒及醬油,並放鹽和糖調味,將芹菜絲加入拌炒數下,再淋下醋與麻油,馬上熄火。
3. 盛入盤中上桌,也可以隨同薄餅或春捲皮一起上桌,以便用來包裹此菜而食。

脆皮八寶鴨
Crispy Duck with Stuffings

材料 >>

鴨1隻（約2公斤重）、糯米飯3杯、冬菇（泡軟、切丁）3個、火腿丁1/4杯、蓮子（泡軟）20粒、筍丁2大匙、青豆1大匙、蝦米（切碎）1大匙、鴨肫1個（切丁）、蔥屑1大匙、油2大匙、炸油 8 杯

調味料 >>

(A) 酒1大匙、淡色醬油2大匙、鹽1/3茶匙、胡椒粉少許

(B) 深色醬油2大匙、麵粉3大匙、蔥屑2大匙、油2大匙、麻油1大匙

做法 >>

1. 將鴨洗淨，從鴨脖子處用刀片割開，順著向下剝皮並割切鴨皮與鴨肉中間之白膜，拆下帶肉的一層，取出鴨之大骨，而仍保持鴨的原狀。
2. 香菇泡軟、切丁，鴨肫也切丁。炒鍋內燒熱2大匙油，先放入蔥屑炒香，再加入各種切丁的材料拌炒，淋下酒1大匙及其他調味料 (A) 等調味，馬上熄火。將糯米飯放下，仔細拌勻。
3. 將糯米飯餡料塞入鴨腹內（8分滿），在開口處需用針線縫合起來（另外如有破裂處亦需縫合），胸部向上平放在盤中，移入鍋中蒸約1小時半。
4. 將蒸好之鴨擦乾水份，全身抹上醬油著色，再均勻地撒下麵粉，放進燒至極熱之油中炸成酥黃為止。
5. 撈起後放在大盤中，先拆除縫線，再在胸部用刀劃切刀口，並在刀口處撒下蔥花。
6. 將炸油2大匙及麻油1大匙在炒鍋內燒熱後，淋在蔥花上使其透出香味，趁熱送席。

Ingredients

- 1 whole duck (about 2kg.)
- 3 cups cooked glutinous rice
- 3 black mushrooms
- 1/4 cup of diced ham
- 20 lotus seeds (soaked)
- 2 tbsp. diced bamboo shoot
- 1 tbsp. green peas (cooked)
- 1 tbsp. chopped dried shrimp (soaked)
- 1 duck gizzard (diced)
- 1 tbsp. chopped green onion
- 2 tbsp. oil
- 8 cups oil for deep fry

Seasonings

(A) 1 tbsp. wine, 2 tbsp. light colored soy sauce, 1/3 tsp. salt, 1/4 tsp.on of black pepper

(B) 2 tbsp. dark colored soy sauce, 3 tbsp. flour, 2 tbsp. chopped green onion, 2 tbsp. oil, 1 tbsp. sesame oil

Procedures

1. Use kitchen scissors or a sharp knife to cut the membranes around the duck's neck. Then stretch and remove all the bones from the duck and keep the duck in its original shape.
2. Soak the black mushrooms to soft and then dice them. Heat 2 tbsp. oil in a frying pan, stir fry the green onion for a few seconds, add the black mushrooms and all the diced ingredients. Sprinkle with wine, and season with seasonings (A). Turn off the heat. Add the cooked glutinous rice and mix thoroughly to make the stuffing.
3. Stuff the stuffing mixture into the cavity of the duck and then seal it with a needle and thread. Put on a platter, steam it over high heat for about 1 1/2 hours.
4. Remove the duck and pat the surface dry. Brush all of the duck skin with dark soy sauce. Then coat it with flour. Deep fry the stuffed duck over high heat until golden brown and crisp.
5. Remove the duck to a platter. Score on the breast side of the duck. Sprinkle 1 tbsp. chopped green onion on the duck.
6. Heat 2 tbsp. oil and 1 tbsp. sesame oil. Pour it over the green onion. Serve immediately.

荷葉粉蒸鴨
Steamed Duck in Lotus Leaves

材料 >>
光鴨半隻（約1公斤）、荷葉2張、蒸肉粉4包（約1 1/2杯）（蒸肉粉做法列入註3.）

醃鴨用料 >>
蔥屑2大匙、薑屑1大匙、醬油2大匙、糖1大匙、酒1大匙、甜麵醬1大匙、油1大匙、麻油1/2大匙

1. 如喜愛辣味，在醃鴨時也可放入1大匙辣椒醬同醃。
2. 用同樣方式可做其他如雞、牛肉、羊肉、排骨、肥腸等粉蒸的菜。
3. 將米1杯（加入少許糯米更佳）放在乾鍋內，加入八角2顆及花椒粒1茶匙，用小火炒黃，待冷後撿去八角等。將米研磨成粗粉狀使可。

做法 >>
1. 將鴨洗淨拭乾水份後，切成3公分寬，5公分長之大小，全部放在盆中，加入蔥等醃鴨調味料充份攪拌均勻，醃約30分鐘（需時常加以上下翻動）。
2. 荷葉洗淨，拭乾水份，分割成6小張（若用乾荷葉，需先洗淨，用溫水泡軟後方可使用）。
3. 鴨肉醃好後，將蒸肉粉撒下與鴨肉調拌均勻，荷葉攤開，上面放一片鴨肉（沾滿蒸肉粉），包裹成長方包，逐個做好後，整齊的排列在蒸碗中。
4. 將包妥之荷葉鴨連碗放入蒸籠中，用大火蒸約2 1/2小時即可取出，倒扣在一只大餐盤內，上桌即成。食時每人一包，攤開在小碟內取食。

Ingredients
1kg. duck
2 pieces lotus leaves (fresh or dried)
1 cup of flavored rice powder

To marinate duck
2 tbsp. chopped green onions
1 tbsp. chopped ginger
2 tbsp. soy sauce
1 tbsp. sugar
1 tbsp. wine
1 tbsp. soy bean paste
1 tbsp. oil
1/2 tbsp. sesame oil

Procedures
1. After cleaning the duck, cut it into 3cm wide, and 5cm long pieces. Put the duck in a large bowl and marinate for about half an hour (turn the duck often while marinating).
2. Cut each lotus leaf into 6 small pieces and then soak with warm water for about 2 hours.
3. Add the rice powder to the duck and mix thoroughly. Place one piece of the duck on a lotus leaf. Fold up the leaf and roll to make a package. Place with smooth side face down on the bottom of a bowl or a deep plate.
4. Steam over high heat for 2 1/2 hours until duck is tender. Put a serving plate upside down over the bowl. Turn the whole thing over so that the duck is on the serving plate. Remove bowl.

1. Each person should unwrap the duck package before eating.
2. Chicken, beef, mutton or pork spareribs can be used instead of duck. You may add some red chili paste in the marinade.
3. To make flavored rice powder by yourself : 1 cup of uncooked rice in a dry pan with 2 star anise and 1 tsp. brown peppercorns. Stir over low heat for 5 minutes until rice gets a little brown. Remove and let cool. Discard the spices. Grind to about the size of bread crumbs.

豬肉篇

豬肉各部份之用途

豬肉係中國人最常吃的肉類，其烹調方法之多，所使用部份之繁，遠較牛肉為多。一般按其部位將較常用之豬肉分割成6大部份：

1. 脊背肉（包括大排骨）：肉質滑嫩而瘦肉多，其中有外脊肉、裡脊肉，可以切片、切丁、切絲、斬絞等，宜做煎、炸、溜、燴等菜之用。
2. 梅肉（包括夾心部份）：瘦多肥少，肉質細嫩，宜製絞肉、做餡及紅燒等用。
3. 小排骨部份：有肥瘦肉、有筋絡，可燜、燒、煎、炸、溜、烤等。
4. 肋條肉（又名五花肉）：肥瘦均有，脂肪層次較多，可紅燒、清嫩、粉蒸、炸、烤等用。
5. 後腿肉部份：瘦多肥少，可做火腿用，也可做絞肉（餡）、紅燒、清燉等菜。
6. 蹄膀（又名肘子）：瘦肉及筋絡較多，宜紅燒、鹽醃、清燉、酒醉等。

About Pork

Chinese people eat more pork than any other meat. There are many different cooking methods for pork. Moreover, the Chinese eat almost every part of the pig. Pork can be divided into 6 major sections:

1. Loin and fat back: Meat is tender. A lot of lean meat. Can be diced, sliced, shredded, and chopped. Can be deep fried, stir fried, braised, sauteed, etc..
2. Shoulder and arm: A lot of lean meat. Very tender. Can be ground and used as stuffing or can be stewed.
3. Spareribs: Has both lean meat and fat. Also has tendons and sinews. Can be stewed, roasted, braised, deep fried, sautéed, simmered.
4. Flank (belly portion): Has both lean meat and fat. Also has layers of fat. Can be braised, stewed, sautéed, steamed, deep fried, baked, etc..
5. Back legs (rump): More lean meat. Can be used as ham or ground meat for stuffing. Also can be braised and stewed.
6. Shank: More fat than lean meat. Can be salted, braised, stewed with wine, etc..

砂鍋獅子頭
Stewed Meatballs in Casserole

材料 >>
半肥瘦豬肉（前腿肉）800公克、大白菜600公克、太白粉1大匙、油1/2杯

拌肉料 >>
蛋1個、酒1大匙、鹽1茶匙、太白粉1大匙、胡椒粉1/8茶匙、蔥薑水1/2杯

調味料 >>
清湯4杯、醬油2大匙、鹽1/3茶匙

 蔥薑水係用蔥支和薑片拍碎浸泡在冷水中，10分鐘後泌出之汁。
To make ginger and green onion juice : Crush 3 slices of ginger and 1 stalk of green onion. Soak in 1/2 cup water for 10 minutes, use the liquid.

做法 >>

1. 把豬肉仔細切成小粒後，再斬剁片刻至肉產生黏性為止，全部裝在大碗內，加入拌肉料，順著同一方向仔細調拌肉料，並擲摔約3分多鐘，致肉有彈性為止。

2. 大白菜先剝下3大片葉子留用，其餘的全部直著切成2.5公分寬之段狀，用油2大匙在鍋內以大火煸炒一下，見已變軟即可盛到砂鍋內鋪平，做墊底之用。

3. 在炒鍋內將油燒熱，將第一項之肉料分為4份，雙手沾少許太白粉水（太白粉加2大匙的水），將每份反覆團弄成一個大丸子狀，輕輕放入油中煎黃兩面，（每面僅10秒鐘即鏟出）移到砂鍋之白菜上，4個全部放好之後，用那3張大白菜葉相疊覆蓋妥當，注入清湯用小火燉煮約3個半小時，如湯汁已不夠時，可在中途酌加熱水。

4. 加入鹽及醬油調味，即可將砂鍋端到飯桌上供食。

Ingredients
800g. pork (25% fat),
600g. napa cabbage,
1 tbsp. cornstarch,
1/2 cup oil

To mix with pork
1 egg,
1 tsp. wine,
1 tsp. salt,
1 1/2 tbsp. cornstarch,
1/8 tsp. black pepper,
1/2 cup of ginger and green onion juice

Seasonings
4 cups of soup stock,
2 tbsp. soy sauce,
1/3 tsp. salt

Procedures
1. Dice the pork, then chop again until it is almost like ground meat. Place the chopped pork in a bowl. Add 1/2 cup of ginger and green onion juice (method refer to the note), and marinades. Stir it with fingers in one direction (never reverse the direction) until they are well mixed. Then take the meat in one hand. Throw it back into the bowl. Repeat this action for about 3 minutes until the pork mixture is very sticky.
2. Remove 3 pieces of cabbage leaf for later use. Cut the rest of the cabbage into pieces about 2.5cm wide. Heat 2 tbsp. oil in a frying pan. Stir fry the cabbage over high heat until soft. Place them on the bottom of a casserole; use them as a mat for the meatballs.
3. Heat 1/2 cup of oil in a pan. Put some cornstarch paste (mix 1 tbsp. cornstarch with 2 tbsp. water) in your palm. Pick up 1/4 of pork mixture and make it into a big meatball. Fry it until it becomes light brown (about 10 seconds on each side). Then put it into the casserole on the cabbage mat. Repeat this procedure until all four meatballs have been made and placed in the casserole. Cover them with the three cabbage leaves. Add the soup stock. Cover the lid. Stew it over low heat for 3 1/2 to 4 hours (if the liquid in the casserole becomes too low while stewing, additional hot soup stock or hot water may be added).
4. Season with the salt and soy sauce. Serve hot.

宮保肉丁

Diced Pork with Dried Hot Peppers

材料 >>
大排骨肉（或全瘦肉）450公克、花生米1/2 杯、乾紅辣椒8支、薑屑1茶匙、油2杯

醃肉料 >>
醬油1大匙、太白粉1/2大匙、水1 1/2 大匙

綜合調味料 >>
醬油1 1/2大匙、酒1大匙、糖1大匙、鎮江醋1/2 大匙、太白粉1茶匙、鹽1/4茶匙、麻油1/2 茶匙

做法 >>

1. 先在肉上用刀背輕輕交叉拍剁之後，再切成約1.5公分大小的四方小塊，用醃肉料拌勻，醃約20分鐘。
2. 生花生米需用開水泡一下（約5分鐘）然後逐粒剝淨澀衣，放進溫油中（約2杯油），以小火慢慢炸熟，撈出吹涼待用（也可買現成之油炸花生米）。
3. 在炒菜鍋中燒熱油2杯（不可太熱，約8分熱—160°C），倒下已醃過之肉丁，用大火迅速炸熟，約20秒鐘即可撈出。
4. 另在炒菜鍋內燒熱2大匙油，先放下切成3公分長段之乾紅辣椒，炸至轉為暗紅色後，再加進薑屑及肉丁，以旺火拌炒數下，隨即倒下調妥之綜合調味料，拌炒均勻，至全部黏稠時，即可將火關熄，加入炸過之花生米，略為拌合即行裝盤供食。

Ingredients
450g. pork tenderloin
1/2 cup of peanuts (raw)
8 dried red chilies
1 tsp. chopped ginger
2 cups of oil

To marinate the pork
1 tbsp. soy sauce
1/2 tbsp. cornstarch
1 1/2 tbsp. water

Seasonings
1 tbsp. soy sauce
1 tbsp. wine
1 tbsp. sugar
1/2 tbsp. brown vinegar
1 tsp. cornstarch
1/4 tsp. salt
1/2 tsp. sesame oil

Procedures
1. Pound the pork with the back of a cleaver. Then cut it into 1.5cm cubes. Marinate for about 20 minutes.
2. Soak the uncooked peanuts in boiling water for about 5 minutes. Remove and peel off the skin. Deep fry the peanuts in warm oil over low heat until light brown. Remove and let cool for later use. (you can use the roasted peanuts, you should remove all salt).
3. Heat 2 cups of oil in a pan (about 160°C). Deep fry the pork cubes over high heat for about 20 seconds. Remove and drain off the oil.
4. Heat another 2 tbsp. oil in the frying pan. Fry the dried red chilies (cut into 3 cm long pieces) for a few seconds until the color turn to more red, add the chopped ginger and the pork. Stir fry over high heat for a few seconds. Pour in the seasoning sauce, mix thoroughly until thickened. Add the deep fried peanuts. Mix well. Serve hot.

荔甫扣肉
Molded Pork with Taro

材料 >>
五花肉600公克、大芋頭1個（約600公克重）深色醬油4大匙、炸油6杯

綜合調味料 >>
酒1大匙、糖1大匙、五香粉少許、蒜頭4粒（切碎）

做法 >>

1. 五花肉要買一整塊方形或長方形，放在鍋中，加水（水要蓋住肉面）用大火煮約30分鐘。
2. 將肉取出，擦乾水份後，泡在深色醬油中，把肉皮泡黑（肉面也需要泡過），放入熱油中去炸，（炸時注意肉皮應朝下放入），見皮炸成褐黃色後翻面再炸，炸到整塊肉已轉為棕色之後便可撈出。
3. 將肉馬上泡到冷水中約30分鐘，至肉皮凸起許多水泡為止。用利刀切成長方大薄片（約6～7公分寬，0.6公分厚）。
4. 芋頭洗淨、去皮，切成同肉塊一樣大之片狀後，用醬油略拌醃一下，再用油炸黃，撈出待用。
5. 預備一個大碗，把肉片和芋頭片相間隔的夾放著，排列在大碗內，多餘的小肉片及芋頭片可放在上面，淋下綜合調味料及所餘下之醬油，加蓋，蒸 2 1/2 小時。
6. 蒸好後，先把湯汁倒出在鍋內煮滾，肉及芋頭全部扣在大盤中，再將湯汁淋到肉面上便可上桌。

Ingredients

600g. pork belly with skin (fresh bacon with rind),
600g. taro,
4 tbsp. dark colored soy sauce,
6 cups oil for deep fry

Seasonings

1 tbsp. wine,
1 tbsp. sugar,
1/4 tsp. five spice powder,
4 garlic buds (chopped)

Procedures

1. Buy the pork in a whole shape. Put it in a pan with water. Boil it over high heat for about 30 minutes.
2. Remove the pork and pat dry the skin. Brush with soy sauce until the pork skin is dark. Deep fry it in very hot oil for about 2 minutes until it is brown. (with skin side on the bottom). Remove.
3. Soak the fried pork in cold water (skin side down) for about 30 minutes until the skin becomes wrinkled and soft. Cut the pork into slices (6~7cm wide and 0.6cm thick).
4. Peel off the skin of taro. Cut it into slices, the same size as the pork. Combine with some soy sauce and then deep fry in very hot oil until it is brown.
5. Arrange the slices of pork and taro in a soup bowl. (the pork and taro side by side). Put the attractive pieces on the bottom and the odd ones in the center. Add the seasonings and remaining soy sauce. Cover and steam over high heat for 2 1/2 hours until tender.
6. Pour the juice from bowl, bring to a boil. Then turn the pork bowl over on a serving plate. Pour the juice over the meat. Serve hot.

京都排骨
Fried Pork Spareribs, Jingdu Style

材料 >>
豬小排骨450公克、炸油4杯

醃肉用料 >>
鹽1/3茶匙、鬆肉粉1/2茶匙或小蘇打1/4茶匙、醬油1大匙、麵粉1大匙、太白粉1大匙、清水2大匙

綜合調味料 >>
油1大匙、A1牛排醬1大匙、辣醬油1大匙、蕃茄醬1大匙、糖1大匙、清水2大匙

做法 >>
1. 小排骨剁成5公分長，再由每支骨頭的中間剖切為兩半（請肉販代為剖切，如不可能則不切也無妨）。
2. 將所有醃肉用料在大碗內調拌妥當之後，放下第一項之小排骨，用手拌勻，醃泡2小時至4小時，使肉變為滑嫩。
3. 在鍋內把炸油燒熱之後，將醃過的小排骨全部放下，用大火炸約3分鐘至呈咖啡色而外層酥脆為止。全部撈出，炸油也倒出。
4. 在鍋內僅用1大匙油，將綜合調味料煮滾，將火關熄，再將小排骨落鍋速加拌合，盛到餐盤內。

Ingredients
450g. pork spareribs,
4 cups oil for deep fry,

To marinate spareribs
1/3 tsp. salt,
1/2 tsp. meat tenderizer (or 1/4tsp. baking soda),
1 tbsp. soy sauce,
1 tbsp. flour,
1 tbsp. cornstarch,
2 tbsp. cold water

Seasoning sauce
1 tbsp. A1 sauce,
1 tbsp. sugar,
1 tbsp. worcestershire sauce,
1 tbsp. ketchup,
2 tbsp. cold water

Procedures
1. Chop the spareribs into 5cm long pieces. Cut the bone lengthwise into two pieces.
2. In a bowl, mix the marinades to marinate the spareribs for 2 to 4 hours.
3. Heat 4 cups of oil in the frying pan until it is very hot. Put all of the spareribs in. Deep fry for about 3 minutes over high heat until they are lightly browned and crispy. Drain.
4. In the sauce pan, boil the seasoning sauce with 1 tbsp. oil. Turn off the heat. Mix the spareribs in. Remove and serve.

豉汁排骨
Spareribs with Fermented Black Beans

材料 >>
小排骨300公克、太白粉1大匙、紅辣椒屑2大匙、大蒜屑2大匙

調味料 >>
豆豉（切碎）2大匙、酒1大匙、鹽1/3茶匙、糖1茶匙、醬油（淡色）1大匙

做法 >>
1. 小排骨連骨及肉斬切成1.5公分寬、2公分長之小塊,和太白粉拌勻。
2. 將豆豉用冷水略沖洗後泡3分鐘,切成小粒備用。
3. 用1大匙油炒香豆豉,並淋下酒爆香,放下鹽、糖和醬油拌勻,關火,放下小排骨拌合均勻。盛出放在碟子上,攤平。
4. 將紅辣椒屑及大蒜屑撒在小排骨上,移入蒸鍋內用大火蒸20分鐘。(鍋中之水應先燒滾)
5. 將蒸好之豉汁排骨另換一個碟子後送上桌供食。

Ingredients

300g. pork spareribs,
1 tbsp. cornstarch,
2 tbsp. chopped hot red pepper,
2 tbsp. chopped garlic

Seasonings

2 tbsp. dried fermented black beans,
1 tbsp. wine,
1/3 tsp. salt,
1 tsp. sugar,
1 tbsp. light colored soy sauce

Procedures

1. Cut chop spareribs into 1.5cm wide, 2 cm long pieces, mix with cornstarch.
2. Soak the fermented black beans for about 3 minutes. Strain off water then chop a little.
3. Heat the oil in a frying pan. Stir fry the fermented black beans over low heat. Add the seasonings. Mix evenly. Turn off the heat, add spareribs in, mix again. Remove to a steaming plate, arrange ribs to a thin layer.
4. Sprinkle chopped red pepper and garlic on top. Steam over high heat for about 20 minutes.
5. Remove and transfer the spareribs to a serving plate. Serve hot.

蒜泥白肉
Sliced Pork with Garlic Sauce

材料 >>
豬後腿肉250公克、黃瓜2條、蔥2支、薑2片

蒜泥醬料 >>
大蒜泥2大匙、鹽1/4茶匙、高湯（冷的）1大匙、醬油膏2大匙、辣油1大匙、麻油半大匙

做法 >>
1. 將豬肉切去皮後，整塊放在水中，加入蔥薑，用中火煮約30分鐘，用筷子試插，如無血水滲出即係已熟，馬上取出，待冷透後用利刀片切成5公分四方大小之薄片（不可順紋切）。
2. 黃瓜切薄片備用。
3. 將肉片全部放在漏勺內，落入開水中，大火快速川燙一下，約5秒鐘即行撈出，瀝乾水份，再用紙巾拭擦一下。
4. 用一只小碗調勻大蒜泥等蒜泥醬料。
5. 將肉片和黃瓜舖排在盤內，再淋上綜合蒜泥醬料便可上桌。

Ingredients
250g. pork (shoulder or ham part)
2 cucumbers
2 stalks green onion
2 slices ginger

Garlic Sauce
2 tbsp. garlic (chopped or mashed)
1/4 tsp. salt
1 tbsp. soup stock (cold)
2 tbsp. soy sauce paste
1 tbsp. hot red pepper oil, 1/2 tbsp. sesame oil

Procedures
1. Rinse the pork and cut off the skin. Cook the whole pork in boiling water with green onion and ginger for about 30 minutes. Poke a chopstick into the pork. If no blood flows out of the hole, the meat is done. Remove and drain. After cooling, slice it across the grain into very thin slices, the size about 5cm square.
2. Slice the cucumbers to the similar size as pork.
3. Boil the pork in boiling water again for only 5 seconds. Remove and drain. Pat dry with a paper towel.
4. Mix garlic sauce in a bowl.
5. Arrange the sliced pork and cucumber on a serving plate. Pour the garlic sauce over the pork. Serve.

豬肉篇
培梅食譜 II

金錢肉
Roast Coin Shaped Pork

材料 >>
大排骨肉（全瘦）600公克、肥肉150公克、蔥2支、薑3片、荷葉夾或土司麵包

醃肉料 >>
五香粉1/4茶匙、糖1 1/2大匙、醬油3大匙、高粱酒1大匙、麻油1/2大匙、胡椒粉少許

註 荷葉夾做法可參考培梅食譜第一冊第324頁。
Refer the "Steamed Flower Shaped Rolls" on Pei-Mei's Chinese Cook Book Volume I, P.324

做法 >>

1. 將整塊大排骨肉用刀切下四邊,使其成為圓筒狀。然後再切成約3.5公分直徑的活頁片(即一刀不斷、第二刀再切斷,成兩片相合之肉片)。肥肉也切成小圓薄片(較瘦肉小一點的)。
2. 將肉全部置大碗內。加入拍碎之蔥、薑及醃肉調味料拌醃1小時。
3. 備2支竹筷子,將一端用刀子修尖待用。
4. 將醃好的每一塊瘦肉中,夾進一片肥肉,全部串在竹筷上(不可靠得太緊),放進已預熱的烤箱中之鐵架子上(約350°F、170°C)。
5. 用中火烤約15分鐘後全部取出(肉不必拿下)、續在泡肉之調味料內再沾上一次或用小刷塗擦也可,換一頭位置,繼續再放入烤箱中,再烤15分鐘。
6. 將烤熟之金錢肉從竹筷上拿下,並刷上少許沙拉油,排列在盤中便成。可附一些糖醋酸果以開胃(吃時用荷葉夾或切了刀口的土司麵包夾食更為理想可口)。

Ingredients

600g. boneless pork loin
150g. pork fat
2 stalks green onion
3 slices ginger
flower shaped rolls or sliced bread

To marinate pork

1/4 tsp. five spice powder
1 1/2 tbsp. sugar
3 tbsp. soy sauce
1 tbsp. wine (gao-liang)
1/2 tbsp. sesame oil
1/4 tsp. black pepper

Procedures

1. Trim the meat into a round shaped about 4 cm diameter. Cut the first slice almost through then cut the second slice completely through. You may get about 15~16 doubled pieces. (The shape should be like a hamburger bun). Cut the pork fat into 15 × 16 round shaped pieces, a little smaller than the lean pork.
2. Place pork and pork fat into a bowl. Add the crushed green onion, ginger, and all marinades. Stir until the ingredients are well mixed. Soak for about one hour.
3. Sharp 2 chopsticks or prepare 2 skewers.
4. Place one slice of fat into the middle of lean pork. Pierce the pork on a skewer. Don't put them too close together. Put the skewers on a baking sheet and place in the oven (preheat to 350ºF、170ºC).
5. Roast the coin shaped pork for 30 minutes at 350ºF. (after roasting for 15 minutes, remove the pork and brush some of the marinade sauce on the pork and then continue to roast).
6. Remove the pork from oven and remove from the skewer. Brush some oil on top. Arrange on a plate, serve with steamed flower shaped rolls or sliced bread.

珍珠丸子
Pearl Balls

材料 >>
絞豬肉450公克、糯米2杯、蝦米屑2大匙、蛋1個、蔥屑1大匙、薑屑1茶匙、太白粉1大匙

調味料 >>
淡色醬油1大匙、鹽1/3茶匙、太白粉1大匙

做法 >>
1. 選購半肥瘦之絞肉，放置在砧板上，再加以剁爛（剁時加入約2大匙清水同剁）然後加入蝦米屑、蔥屑、薑屑、調味料及蛋，用力拌攪，調好成為肉餡。
2. 糯米洗淨，泡約半小時，瀝乾水份，並用紙巾盡量吸乾水份。
3. 在一個托盤上撒下另外1大匙太白粉，將糯米鋪上，略拌合一下。將第一項之肉餡抓在左手中，撥弄大姆指捏擠出適當大小之肉丸，用湯匙取下，放在糯米上面（可做24個普通大小丸子）。
4. 搖動托盤，使肉丸上滾滿糯米，然後再將丸子一個個握在手掌中捏圓，放到鋪了濕布的蒸籠內，用大火蒸約20～25分鐘便成。
5. 趁熱夾出，排在盤內上桌供食。

Ingredients
450g ground pork, 2 cups glutinous rice, 2 tbsp. chopped dry shrimp, 1 egg, 1 tbsp. chopped green onion, 1 tsp. chopped ginger, 1 tbsp. cornstarch

Seasonings
1 tbsp. lighted soy sauce,
1/3 tsp. salt,
1 tbsp. cornstarch

Procedures
1. Chop the ground pork with 2 tbsp. cold water. Place the pork in a bowl. Add the chopped dry shrimp, (soaked first to soften), chopped green onion, chopped ginger, egg and seasonings. Mix well until the pork is very sticky.
2. Rinse the glutinous rice and soak in cold water for about half an hour. Drain and wipe dry with a paper towel.
3. Sprinkle 1 tbsp. cornstarch on a tray, mix with the glutinous rice. Wet your left hand, hold the pork mixture in your palm sgueeze out a meatball, the size about a walnut, remove the ball with a wet spoon, and put it on the glutinous rice. Make about 24 meatballs.
4. Roll and rock the tray back and forth so that the glutinous rice will stick to all sides of the meatballs. Afterwards, put the ball in your palm. Roll each ball in your palm lightly until it is round enough. Then place meatballs in a steamer on a damp cloth and steam for about 20~25 minutes over high heat.
5. Remove to a serving plate and serve hot.

蔥串排骨
Stuffed Spareribs with Brown Sauce

材料 >>
小排骨900公克、蔥白（約6～7公分長）15支、蔥2支、薑3片

調味料 >>
酒1大匙、醬油5大匙、糖2大匙、開水3杯、鎮江醋1大匙、麻油1茶匙

做法 >>
1. 選購平整而骨頭直之小排骨，剁成4公分長，用3大匙油爆炒1分鐘（需加入蔥、薑同炒），淋下酒及醬油，並放下糖及清水，蓋好鍋蓋用中火煮約半小時左右，至湯汁剩下1杯為止。
2. 淋下醋到鍋中繼續煮1分鐘，即將排骨撈出，然後將每條排骨中之骨頭抽出，換進1支約7公分長之蔥白。
3. 待全部換好後，重倒回鍋內，再用小火煮1分鐘。淋下麻油即可盛到盤內（應略加排列整齊）。

Ingredients
900g. pork spareribs,
15 pieces green onion (white part about 7cm long),
2 stalks green onion,
3 slices ginger

Seasonings
1 tbsp. wine,
5 tbsp. soy sauce,
2 tbsp. sugar,
3 cups hot water,
1 tbsp. vinegar,
1 tsp. sesame oil

Procedures
1. Cut each piece of sparerib into 4cm long pieces. Heat 3 tbsp. oil to stir fry the spareribs, green onion, and ginger for about 1 minute. Splash in the wine, soy sauce, sugar and water. Cover the lid, and stew over low heat for about 1/2 hour until the sauce is reduced to 1 cup.
2. Splash in vinegar and cook for 1 more minute. Remove the spareribs. Then pull out the bone from each of the sparerib. In place of the bone, put in one piece of green onion.
3. Return all of the stuffed spareribs to pan. stew with the remaining sauce for about 1 minute again. Splash in sesame oil. Remove to a serving plate and serve.

京醬肉絲
Stir-fried Pork with Bean Sauce

材料 >>
瘦肉300公克、大蔥絲1 1/2杯、油2杯、薄餅或春捲皮20張

醃肉料 >>
醬油1大匙、太白粉1大匙、水1 1/2大匙

甜麵醬料 >>
甜麵醬2大匙、糖2茶匙、水1大匙

Ingredients
300g. pork tenderloin,
1 1/2 cups shredded green onion,
2 cups oil,
20 pieces dan-bing or egg roll wrapper

To marinate pork
1 tbsp. soy sauce,
1 tbsp. cornstarch,
1 1/2 tbsp. cold water

Bean sauce
2 tbsp. sweet soy bean paste,
2 tsp. sugar,
1 tbsp. water

Procedures
1. Shred pork into long and thin strips (about 4cm long). Marinate for 30 minutes. (Use your fingers or chopsticks to mix until thoroughly combined).
2. Put the shredded green onion on a plate.
3. Heat oil to 300°F(140°C). Add pork strings and stir fry for 15 seconds until done. Remove and put aside. Drain off oil from the pan.
4. Heat 2 tbsp. oil in the same pan. Fry the mixed bean sauce until fragrant and looks shining. Add pork. Stir thoroughly. Remove to the plate and put over the green onions.
5. Before eating, mix pork and green onions well. Then roll it up in a egg roll wrapper or dan- bing.

1. 薄餅（又名單餅）做法在培梅食譜第一冊318頁。
2. 沒有大蔥時可用一般的蔥，大蔥較為脆甜。
1. Refer the recipe for dan-bing on Pei-Mei's Chinese Cook Book Volume 1, p. 318.
2. It is better to use scallion the green onion. scallion is more crispier

做法 >>

1. 將豬肉全部切成細絲（約4公分長），用醃肉料拌勻，醃泡半小時左右。
2. 大蔥斜切成長約4公分的細絲，全部舖在菜盤中備用。
3. 將2杯油在炒鍋中燒至七分熱後傾下拌醃過之豬肉絲泡炸，用筷子迅速撥散，見肉絲變色（約15秒鐘）即行撈出並瀝乾，餘油倒出。
4. 另在炒鍋內燒熱2大匙油，倒下已調勻之甜麵醬料，爆炒至有香味並光滑發亮時，再加入肉絲拌炒，隨即盛在盤中大蔥絲上，即可上桌。
5. 食時需與蔥絲調拌均勻，則蔥亦成半熟狀，用春捲皮或薄餅捲裹包食之。

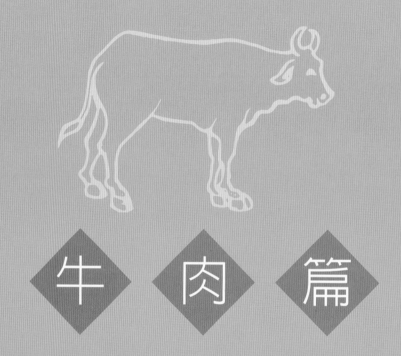

牛肉篇

牛肉各部份之用途

牛肉之脂肪成分少於豬肉，本是西菜中用途較多之肉類，但近年來嗜好牛肉之中國人也愈來愈多，而新式之烹調方法也正增列在菜單與食譜上。牛肉之各部位的分割方式，與西方分割法略有不同（西方分得詳細而名稱多，又有許多部份連骨同切），我們常用的部份，大體上可分為下列數種：

1. 脊背（包括裡脊肉和肩胛肉）：肉質細嫩，無論炸、炒、爆、溜、川均可。
2. 頸肉：適於紅燒、醬滷以及絞碎做餡用。
3. 前腿肉：除極小部份較老之外，大部份均可用做煎、炒、炸、爆、溜、川等用。
4. 肋條部份：相等於豬之五花肉，有筋絡及脂肪層，宜紅燒、燜、燉、煮湯等用。
5. 肚腩（又名牛腩）：係一扁平而肉薄、且帶白筋之部份，適合燒、燉、煮湯等用。
6. 牛尾：由16個關節所連接而成，連皮分割後燒、燉或煨湯，富膠質，香膩可口為高級之菜餚。

About Beef

In recent years, many Chinese also have developed a taste for beef. With this development, new recipes and methods of cooking have appeared. The Chinese divide beef into different and fewer sections than westerns do:

1. Short loin and sirloin: Is juicy and tender. Can be deep fried, stir fried, quick stir fried, sautéed, fried, boiled, etc..
2. Neck: Can be braised, cooked with soy sauce, and ground for stuffing.
3. Brisket: A small part is tough, but the rest of it can be fried, stir fried, deep fried, quick stir fried, braised, etc..
4. Short rib: Similar to bacon in pork. Has layers of tendons and sinews intermixed with fat.
5. Foreshank and shank: Is tough and has a lot of tendons and sinews. Can be stewed or braised for a long time.
6. Tail: 16 joints altogether. Remove the skin and cut into pieces. Can be stewed, braised, or used to make soup. Has a lot of elasticity and a good smell.

家常小牛排
Beef Steak, Home Style

材料 >>
嫩牛肉450公克、蔥屑1大匙、豌豆片（或芥蘭菜）200公克、鹽1/3茶匙

蔥薑水 >>
蔥2支、薑3片、酒1/2大匙、清水4大匙

醃牛肉料 >>
胡椒粉1/4茶匙、醬油1大匙、嫩精1/2茶匙（或小蘇打1/4茶匙）、麵粉1大匙、太白粉1大匙

綜合調味料 >>
醬油1大匙、蕃茄醬1大匙、辣醬油1大匙、糖2茶匙、太白粉1茶匙、水3大匙

做法 >>
1. 牛肉用利刀橫面（逆紋）切成約4公分直徑、0.6公分厚之圓片，每片再用刀面或肉槌拍扁、打鬆。
2. 蔥、薑拍碎，放小碗內，加入酒及清水浸泡10分鐘，丟棄蔥、薑（此汁即稱蔥薑水）。
3. 將醃牛肉料與蔥薑水混合調勻，放進牛肉片醃泡2小時。
4. 鍋內燒熱1/2杯油，投下牛肉片，用大火炸約20秒、見牛肉將熟時即撈出、瀝乾油。
5. 另用1大匙油煮滾綜合調味料，熄火後，將牛肉片和蔥花落鍋，略加拌合即裝盤。
6. 用1大匙油炒摘好的豌豆片，加鹽調味，盛盤中隨牛排上桌。

Ingredients
450g. beef tenderloin, 1 tbsp. chopped green onion, 200g. snow pea pots, 1/3 tsp. salt

To make green onion & ginger juice
2 stalks green onion, 3 slices ginger, 1/2 tbsp. wine, 4 tbsp. cold water

To marinate the beef
1/4 tsp. black pepper, 1 tbsp. soy sauce, 1/2 tsp. meat tenderizer or 1/5 tsp. baking soda, 1 tbsp. flour, 1 tbsp. cornstarch

Seasonings sauce
1 tbsp. soy sauce, 1 tbsp. ketchup, 1 tbsp. worcestershire sauce, 2 tsp. sugar, 1 tsp. cornstarch, 3 tbsp. water

Procedures
1. Cut the beef across the grain into 0.6cm thick and 4cm diameter round pieces. Pound each piece of beef several times with a meat mallet or the back of a knife.
2. Crush the green onion and ginger. Mix with wine and water, soak for 10 minutes to make the green onion and ginger juice.
3. In a bowl, mix the marinades with the green onion and ginger juice first, and then add beef, mix well, soak for at least 2 hours.
4. Heat 1/2 cup of oil in a pan. Deep fry the steak over high heat for 20 seconds till just cooked. Remove and drain off the oil.
5. Return 1 tbsp. oil to the same pan. Pour in the seasoning sauce and bring it to a boil. Turn off the heat. Put the steak and chopped green onion into the sauce, mix well. Remove to a serving platter.
6. Stir fry the snow pea pots with 1 tbsp. oil and season with salt. Serve with the steak.

咖哩牛肉片
Sliced Beef with Curry Sauce

材料 >>
嫩牛肉200公克、洋蔥丁1杯、馬鈴薯400公克、胡蘿蔔片20小片

醃牛肉料 >>
淡色醬油1大匙、太白粉1/2大匙、糖1茶匙、水1大匙

調味料 >>
咖哩粉1 1/2大匙、清水2杯、鹽2/3茶匙、糖1茶匙

做法 >>
1. 牛肉選購無筋而細紋之全瘦肉,用利刀逆紋切成3公分四方薄片,用醃肉料拌醃半小時以上(時間醃得久比較嫩),臨下鍋前再拌上1大匙油。
2. 馬鈴薯削皮後切滾刀片;洋蔥切小丁備用。
3. 鍋燒熱,用2大匙油炒香洋蔥,再加入咖哩粉同炒,然後放下馬鈴薯及胡蘿蔔片,用大火炒數秒鐘,隨即加水2杯,並下鹽和糖,蓋好鍋蓋、煮約10分鐘至馬鈴薯夠爛為止。
4. 將醃好的牛肉片,一片片攤開平擺在鍋內,再蓋好鍋蓋、以大火煮約10〜15秒鐘,揭開鍋蓋,再淋下1大匙熱油,便可熄火略為拌合一下,馬上盛在盤中。

Ingredients
200g. beef (tenderloin or flank steak), 1 cup diced onion, 400g. potatoes, 20 slices carrot

To marinate the beef
1 tbsp. light colored soy sauce, 1/2 tbsp. cornstarch, 1 tsp. sugar, 1 tbsp.cold water

Seasonings
1 1/2 tbsp. curry powder, 2 cups cold water, 2/3 tsp. salt, 1 tsp. sugar

Procedures
1. Cut the beef into 3 cm square thin slices (across the grain). Mix with marinades for 1/2 hour at least (longer is better). Add 1 tbsp. oil and mix well before cooking.
2. Cut the potatoes into diagonal pieces.
3. Heat 2 tbsp. oil. Stir fry the onion. Add the curry powder, then carrot and potatoes. Stir fry for a while. Add 2 cups of cold water. Season with salt and sugar. Cover the lid and reduce the heat to low, cook for about 10 minutes.
4. Place all of the beef slices by slice on top of the curry sauce. Cover and cook over high heat for about 10~15 seconds. Splash 1 tbsp. heated oil. Turn off the heat. Remove to a platter.

 此菜也可將牛肉先用熱油過油,待熟後撈出,再放入鍋中煮好之咖哩材料內拌勻。
You may stir fry the beef for about 10 seconds until done, and then mix with the curry sauce.

玉蘭炒牛肉
Sliced Beef with Broccoli

材料 >>
嫩牛肉250公克、油1大匙、芥蘭菜200公克、蔥段（1.5公分長）15段、薑片15片、炸油1杯

醃牛肉料 >>
糖1/2茶匙、醬油1/2大匙、小蘇打1/5茶匙、太白粉2茶匙、清水1大匙

綜合調味料 >>
醬油1/2大匙、蠔油2大匙、酒1/2大匙、糖1茶匙、太白粉1/2茶匙

做法 >>
1. 將牛肉橫紋切成約2.5公分四方大小之薄片後，用醃肉料拌勻，臨下鍋前，放置半小時以上再淋下1大匙油調好。
2. 小碗內將綜合調味料調好留用。
3. 芥蘭菜摘短成約3公分長段，並撕去老筋，用開水燙煮半分鐘，撈出後沖過冷水、瀝乾。
4. 用炸油將牛肉片過油炒熟（油不可太熱，僅炒10秒鐘即熟），瀝乾油漬，而將鍋中油也倒出。
5. 另燒熱3大匙油在炒鍋內，先炒香蔥、薑，並放下芥蘭菜同炒，約10秒鐘後，將牛肉片落鍋，並馬上將綜合調味料也倒下，以大火拌炒勻便可關火裝盤。

Procedures

1. Slice the beef across the grain into 2.5 cm square slices. Place in a bowl. Mix well with marinades first. Then add 1 tbsp. oil and marinate it for half an hour at least.
2. In a small bowl, mix the seasoning sauce.
3. Trim the mustard green into 3 cm long pieces. Boil it in boiling water for 30 seconds. Remove and plunge into the cold water. Then drain and dry.
4. Heat the oil in a frying pan to about 300°F (140°C). Stir fry the beef for 10 seconds until it is done. Remove the beef and drain off oil.
5. Heat another 2 tbsp. oil in the same pan to stir fry the green onion and ginger for a few seconds. Add the mustard green, stir fry for about 10 seconds, add the beef and the seasoning sauce. Stir quickly over high heat until mixed. Remove to a platter and serve hot.

Ingredients

250g. beef tenderloin,
1 tbsp. oil,
200g. mustard green (or broccoli),
15 pieces green onion,
15 slices ginger,
1 cup oil for deep fry

To marinate the beef

1/2 tsp. sugar,
1/2 tbsp. soy sauce,
1/5 tsp. baking soda,
2 tsp. cornstarch,
1 tbsp. cold water

Seasonings sauce

1/2 tbsp. soy sauce,
2 tbsp. oyster sauce,
1/2 tbsp. wine,
1tsp. sugar,
1/2 tsp. cornstarch

中式牛肉餅
Stewed Meatballs, Chinese Style

材料 >>
絞牛肉400公克、絞肥豬肉80公克、水3大匙、油1/2杯、大白菜600公克、鹽1/3茶匙、清湯1杯、蔥屑1大匙

拌牛肉料 >>
薑汁1茶匙、蛋1個、小蘇打1/4茶匙、淡色醬油1/2大匙、鹽1/4茶匙、酒1/2大匙、太白粉1大匙

調味料 >>
醬油1大匙、鹽1/4茶匙、糖1/2茶匙、太白粉水2茶匙、麻油1/2茶匙

做法 >>

1. 將絞牛肉及肥豬肉置菜板上加入冷水3大匙後,用刀重行剁爛(一分鐘),然後裝在大碗內,放入拌牛肉料,仔細拌攪至牛肉生黏性而極勻滑為止。
2. 大白菜切長段後,用油2大匙,炒熟,加鹽1/3茶匙調味,盛入盤中。
3. 將1/2杯油在鍋內燒熱後,用左手抓住牛肉餡,從大姆指與食指中間擠出圓形丸子投入鍋內,待全部放下後,用鏟子將牛肉丸壓扁,使成為小肉餅狀,用慢火煎黃兩面,將多餘的油盛出。
4. 注入清湯1杯,並加醬油、鹽和糖調味,用小火煮約2分鐘。
5. 用調了水之太白粉勾芡,成稍黏稠狀後,淋下麻油少許,撒上蔥花即可盛入大盤中之白菜上供食。

Procedures

1. Chop the beef and pork fat with 3 tbsp. cold water for about 1 minute until very fine. Place in a bowl. Add seasonings A, mix together with your fingers or chopsticks until the ingredients are thoroughly combined and smooth.
2. Cut the cabbage into large pieces. Stir fry with 2 tbsp. oil. Season with 1/3 tsp. salt. Cover and cook until cabbage is soft. Remove to a platter.
3. Heat 1/2 cup of oil in a pan. Wet left hand and place 2 or 3 tbsp. beef mixture in your palm, close fingers to make a meatball. With a wet spoon (use right hand) remove the ball and put it in hot oil. After putting all meatballs in the oil, press the meatballs slightly flat with a spatula. Fry both sides until golden brown. Drain off the oil from the pan.
4. Pour 1 cup of soup stock into the pan. Add soy sauce, salt and sugar. Cover and cook over low heat for 2 minutes. Thicken the sauce with cornstarch paste. Splash sesame oil and chopped green onion on top. Transfer to the platter and place over stir fried cabbage.

Ingredients

400g. ground beef,
80g. ground pork fat,
3 tbsp. cold water,
1/2 cup oil,
600g. napa cabbage,
1/3 tsp. salt,
1 cup soup stock,
1 tbsp. chopped green onion

Seasonings (A)

1 tsp. ginger juice,
1 egg,
1/4 tsp. baking soda,
1/2 tbsp. light colored soy sauce,
1/4 tsp. salt,
1/2 tbsp. wine,
1 tbsp. cornstarch

Seasonings (B)

1 tbsp. soy sauce,
1/4 tsp. salt,
1/2 tsp. sugar,
2 tsp. cornstarch paste,
1/2 tsp. sesame oil

紅燒牛腩
Stewed Beef in Casserole

材料 >>

牛腩1公斤、熱水10杯、油3大匙、大蒜4粒、薑5片、白蘿蔔（或大白菜）600公克、油2大匙

調味料 >>

酒6大匙、醬油1杯、糖1大匙、八角2顆

做法 >>

1. 先將牛腩洗淨，整塊放入鍋中，用開水10杯煮約半小時（小火），撈出待稍冷後切成5公分長，2.5公分寬，1公分厚的大塊。
2. 在炒鍋中用2大匙油先爆香大蒜粒及薑片，淋入酒，續加入醬油、糖、八角以及上項之牛肉湯和牛肉塊，蓋鍋、燒煮至沸滾即改用小火燜煮約1 1/2小時。
3. 將蘿蔔切成與牛肉大小相同之塊後，放在砂鍋中內，再將煮過的牛肉倒進砂鍋中，續用小火煨煮約半小時。
4. 上桌前，在炒鍋中燒熱1大匙油淋到牛肉上，則既光亮又可保溫（也可以撒下少許蔥花或青蒜絲增加香氣）。

Ingredients

1kg. beef (brisket),
10 cups hot water,
3 tbsp. oil,
4 garlic buds,
5 slices ginger,
600g. turnips (or napa cabbage),
2 tbsp. oil

Seasonings

6 tbsp. wine,
1 cup of soy sauce,
1 tbsp. sugar,
2 star anise

Procedures

1. Rinse the beef and cook it in 10 cups of boiling water for 1/2 hour over low heat. Remove it and let it cool. Slice the beef into pieces, about 5cm long, 2.5cm wide, 1cm thick.
2. Heat 2 tbsp. oil in a frying pan. Fry garlic and ginger slices for a few seconds. Then add the seasonings and the cooked beef with beef soup. Cover the pan and bring to a boil. Reduce the heat, stew for 1 1/2 hours.
3. Slice the turnip into pieces about the same size as the beef. Place the turnip on the bottom of a casserole, then pour the beef over the turnips. Stew over low heat for 1/2 hour.
4. Heat 1 tbsp. oil in a frying pan, pour it over the beef (it gives the beef a brilliance and will keep it warm as well) and serve.

蔥爆牛肉
Quick Stir-fried Beef with Green onion

材料 >>
火鍋牛肉片250公克、大蔥絲2杯、大蒜片3大匙、油4大匙

醃牛肉料 >>
鹽1/4茶匙、酒1/2大匙、油1大匙、胡椒粉1/6茶匙、水1大匙、太白粉1/2大匙

調味料 >>
醬油1大匙、麻油1茶匙

Ingredients
250g. sliced beef,
2 cups shredded green onion,
3 tbsp. sliced garlic,
4 tbsp. oil

To marinate beef
1/4 tsp. salt,
1/2 tbsp. wine,
1 tbsp. oil,
1/6 tsp. black pepper,
1 tbsp. cold water,
1/2 tbsp. cornstarch

Seasonings
1 tbsp. soy sauce,
1 tsp. sesame oil

Procedures
1. Prepare the beef marinade in a bowl. Then add the sliced beef (the beef slices must be paper thin). Mix thoroughly with your fingers. Set aside and marinate at least for 10 minutes.
2. Heat oil in a pan. Turn the pan around so that the oil covers about 1 foot diameter.
3. When the oil is smoking hot, put the sliced garlic in. Then add the sliced beef. Stir over high heat for about 10 seconds. Splash soy sauce around the sides of the pan. Mix and remove to a bowl. Reserve the juice in pan.
4. Reheat the juice; then add green onion, stir fry only for 5 seconds. Turn off the heat. Pour the beef back into the pan. Combine with green onion and add sesame oil. Transfer to a serving plate.

做法 >>

1. 牛肉以每片不超過5公分長方大小為準，全部放在大碗內，加入醃肉用料仔細用手調拌均勻，放置10分鐘以上。
2. 把炒菜鍋燒得極熱之後將油放下，提起鍋子燙一下，使油的面積擴大。
3. 見油已燒得極熱（冒煙）時，將蒜片下鍋，馬上將牛肉片落鍋大火急速鏟炒約10秒鐘，見肉片轉色並已脫生時，由鍋邊淋下醬油，即全部鏟出。汁仍留鍋內。
4. 將留在鍋中之汁（油）再燒熱一下，將蔥絲倒下，大火炒5秒鐘，即將火關熄，然後將鏟出之牛肉片合入拌勻，淋下麻油儘快裝碟供食。

滑蛋牛肉
Scrambled Eggs with Beef Slices

材料 >>
嫩牛肉120公克、油1大匙、蛋5個、鹽1/3茶匙、油1杯、蔥粒2大匙

醃牛肉料 >>
薑汁1/4茶匙、嫩精1/2茶匙、糖1/2茶匙、酒1/2大匙、太白粉1大匙、淡色醬油1大匙、清水2大匙

Ingredients

120g. beef tenderloin (or flank steak),
5 eggs,
1/3 tsp. salt,
1 cup oil,
2 tbsp. chopped green onion,

To marinate beef

1/4 tsp. ginger juice or ginger powder,
1/2 tsp. meat tenderizer,
1/2 tsp. sugar,
1/2 tbsp. wine,
1 tbsp. cornstarch,
1 tbsp. light colored soy sauce,
2 tbsp. cold water,

Procedures

1. Cut the beef into 3cm slices (against the grain). Marinate the beef with the mixed marinades. Turn them over occasionally and marinate for at least 30 minutes. Add 1 tbsp. oil to beef just before stir-fry it.
2. Beat the eggs with 1/3 tsp. salt.
3. Set a Chinese wok or frying pan over high heat for about 20 seconds. Pour in 1 cup of oil and heat it to very hot. Add the beef and stir fry until the color turns light (about 10 seconds). Remove beef and drain off the oil. Mix beef with beaten eggs.
4. Heat another 4 tbsp. oil to stir fry the chopped green onion, then pour all of the egg mixture in to the pan. Stir for a few seconds until the eggs are almost cooked, remove the egg quickly.

做法 >>

1. 牛肉切成約3公分四方大小之薄片（注意不可順紋切）然後放在已經調勻的醃肉料中仔細拌勻，醃半小時以上。在下鍋前加入1大匙油，再行調拌均勻。
2. 蛋5個在大碗內加鹽打散至均勻為止。
3. 將炒鍋燒熱後，傾入油1杯，待油溫達到9成熱時即將牛肉片落鍋，用大火急炒，見肉色變淡而熟時即行撈起瀝乾，倒進蛋碗內與蛋汁拌合。
4. 另在炒鍋內燒熱4大匙油，先將蔥粒下鍋，隨將牛肉蛋汁也傾下，用大火急加拌炒，至蛋汁成為半凝固狀態時，便可迅速盛出，裝盤上桌。

魚香牛肉絲
Stir-fried Beef with Hot Sauce

註 "魚香"係指四川菜中燒魚時所用之各種佐料而言，此也即係四川菜之代表口味。

You may deep fry the beef for about 3 seconds and then mix with the curry sauce.

材料 >>
嫩牛肉300公克、荸薺6個、乾木耳2大匙、薑屑2茶匙、蒜屑1茶匙、辣豆瓣醬1大匙、蔥屑2大匙

醃牛肉料 >>
醬油1大匙、太白粉1大匙、糖1/2茶匙、水1大匙、油1大匙

綜合調味料 >>
醬油1大匙、鎮江醋1/2大匙、酒1/2大匙、糖1茶匙、鹽1/4茶匙、太白粉2茶匙、麻油1茶匙、胡椒粉少許

做法 >>
1. 將牛肉逆紋切薄片後,再切成約4公分長之細絲,用醃肉料拌勻,再加入油調好,醃約10分鐘以上。
2. 木耳用溫水泡軟,摘去根蒂、洗淨,切成細絲;荸薺去皮、洗淨,也切絲備用。
3. 鍋中燒熱油2杯(約8分熱),傾入醃過之牛肉絲過油,迅速用筷子撥散,見肉絲變色已致熟時隨即撈起,餘油倒出。
4. 另在炒菜鍋內燒熱2大匙油,先爆炒薑屑、蒜屑與辣豆瓣醬,至顏色鮮紅時,放下荸薺絲與木耳絲同炒,然後將牛肉絲合入拌炒數下,隨後即倒下綜合調味料,以大火迅速拌炒均勻至汁黏稠為止,撒下蔥屑,裝盤趁熱供食。

Ingredients
300g. beef tenderloin, 6 water chestnuts, 2 tbsp. dried black fungus, 2 tsp. chopped ginger, 1 tsp. chopped garlic, 1 tbsp. hot bean paste or chili sauce, 2 tbsp. chopped green onion

To marinate beef
1 tbsp. soy sauce, 1 tbsp. cornstarch, 1/2 tsp. sugar, 1 tbsp. cold water, 1 tbsp. oil

Seasoning sauce
1 tbsp. soy sauce, 1/2 tbsp. vinegar, 1/2 tbsp. wine, 1 tsp. sugar, 1/4 tsp. salt, 2 tsp. cornstarch, 1 tsp. sesame oil, 1/4 tsp. black pepper

Procedures
1. Cut the beef into shreds (match stick size). Mix evenly with marinades, stay at least for 10 minutes.
2. Soak the black fungus with warm water to soft, cut them into shreds. Peel the water chestnuts. Cut into shreds.
3. Heat 2 cups of oil to 160ºC. Add beef and stir until the color changes. Remove and drain.
4. Return the pan to the heat and add 2 tbsp. oil to the pan. Stir fry the ginger, garlic, and hot bean paste. When the oil turns red, add the water chestnuts, fungus, and beef. Stir fry for a few seconds and then add the seasoning sauce. Mix it thoroughly. Turn off heat and sprinkle the chopped green onion. Serve.

紙包牛肉
Paper-wrapped Beef

材料 >>
嫩牛肉150公克、芹菜屑2大匙、胡蘿蔔小片（煮熟）14小片、洋蔥屑2大匙、玻璃紙1大張、麻油2茶匙、炸油6杯

醃牛肉料 >>
淡色醬油2大匙、酒1大匙、糖1茶匙、小蘇打1/6茶匙、胡椒粉少許、油1大匙

做法 >>

1. 將牛肉橫紋切成大薄片（約3.5公分寬，5公分長）用醃牛肉料拌勻，醃約半小時（需時時加以翻動）。
2. 將玻璃紙剪成約15公分四方形，每張在中間部位刷上少許麻油，然後放少許芹菜屑及洋蔥屑與一片胡蘿蔔片在中央部位，再平放一片醃過的牛肉，然後折疊四角，包裹成長方形。
3. 用多量溫熱的炸油，將包妥之牛肉包炸熟（用小火炸約15秒鐘）用漏勺撈出、瀝乾餘油，即可排列在菜盤中。

Ingredients
150g. beef tenderloin, 2 tbsp. chopped celery, 14 pieces cooked carrot, 2 tbsp. chopped onion, 1 piece of cellophane paper, 2 tsp. sesame oil, 6 cups oil for deep fry

To marinate beef
2 tbsp. soy sauce, 1 tbsp. wine, 1 tsp. sugar, 1/6 tsp. baking soda, a pinch black pepper, 1 tbsp. oil

Procedures

1. Slice the beef across the grain into 3.5cm wide, and 5cm long thin slices. Place in a bowl. Marinate for at least 1/2 hour (stir it frequently while marinating).
2. Cut the paper to 15 × 15 cm squares, brush the center part with some sesame oil. Put some chopped celery, onion and one slice of carrot on it and then put 1 slice of beef on top. Fold up the corners to make a package.
3. Heat the oil in a pan to about 150°C. Deep fry the beef packages over low heat for 10 seconds. Remove and arrange on a platter and serve hot.

牛肉篇
培梅食譜 II

紅燴牛尾

Stewed Ox Tail, Chinese Style

材料 >>
牛尾1公斤、蕃茄（切塊）3杯、清水6杯、洋蔥塊1杯、胡蘿蔔厚片1/2杯、麵粉2大匙

調味料 >>
酒1大匙、醬油2大匙、鹽1茶匙、蕃茄醬3大匙

做法 >>

1. 將已切成小段之牛尾,先用滾水浸泡5分鐘,刷洗乾淨,然後放進平底深鍋中,加入1杯切成塊之蕃茄,並注入清水6杯,淋下1大匙酒,用小火燉煮至牛尾酥爛為止。(約3小時)
2. 在炒鍋內燒熱3大匙油,先炒香洋蔥塊,再加入胡蘿蔔厚片及2杯蕃茄塊同炒,並加入第一項之牛尾湯1杯,再用小火燜煮至胡蘿蔔片已軟為止。
3. 另在鍋內加熱3大匙油,加入2大匙麵粉用小火炒勻,加入2杯牛尾湯,迅速調拌使成糊狀,再放其餘調味料拌勻。
4. 將第2項之蔬菜全部傾入湯汁中,用小火同煮3分鐘。
5. 將第1項已煮爛之牛尾塊放進上項材料中,略加拌合並再煮3分鐘,即可裝盤趁熱上桌。

Ingredients

1kg. ox tail,
3 cups tomatoes cubes,
6 cups cold water,
1 cup diced onion,
1/2 cup sliced carrot,
2 tbsp. flour

Seasonings

1 tbsp. wine,
2 tbsp. soy sauce,
1 tsp. salt,
3 tbsp. ketchup

Procedures

1. Cut the ox tail into sections according to its cartilage. Soak the ox tail in boiling water for about 5 minutes. Then brush and clean it. Put them in a pan. Add 1 cup of tomatoes, 6 cups of water (enough to cover the ox tail) and 1 tbsp. wine. Cover. Stew for about 3 hours over low heat until tender.
2. Heat 3 tbsp. oil in a frying pan. Fry the onion cubes for a while. Then add the carrot and remaining tomato cubes. Stir fry for a few minutes. Add 1 cup of beef soup (from No. 1). Stew over low heat until the carrot is soft.
3. Heat another 3 tbsp. oil in a frying pan, add the flour and fry for a few seconds. Then add 2 cups of the ox tail soup (prepared in No. 1). Mix thoroughly until it becomes a paste. Add other seasonings in.
4. Pour No. 2 vegetables into No. 3 paste. Stew together over low heat for about 3 minutes.
5. Add the prepared ox tail; boil again for about 3 minutes. Remove to a platter and serve.

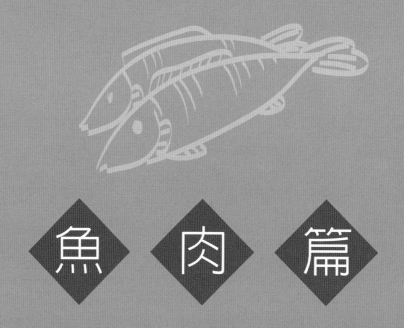

魚肉篇

有關魚類

魚分為海水魚及淡水魚2大類,而淡水魚又分為養殖魚與天然野生魚。在中國宴席上,魚是不可缺少的一道主菜,通常都被列在最後,於甜點之前上席,不但象徵著"吉慶有餘"(豐富有餘),也意味著主菜已上完,宴席即將結束之意。在宴席上所用之魚,一向採用整條形狀之全魚,以表示禮貌與敬意(有頭有尾、十全十美之意),但近年來為考慮食用者取食之方便起見,已逐漸改為去骨或切片、切條等僅採用局部魚肉加以烹調之菜式。

魚之烹調方法很多,一般家庭可行之途有:紅燒、乾煎、酥炸、清蒸、溜、炒、烤、燻等數種。由於魚肉本身係清淡而具鮮味之材料,是故無論如何烹調,均應先加以短時間之醃泡過程為佳。魚皮所含之膠質成份較多,在煎、炸時極易黏粘鍋底,防止方法可將鍋乾燒得極熱之後,用薑片拭擦,再放油下鍋,待油燒熱之後,再將魚下鍋便可。

About Fish

Fish are divided into salt water fish and fresh water fish. In Chinese cooking, fish is considered to be one of the most important dishes. Usually, it is the last major dish served before the dessert. This is due to the fact that the Chinese sound for "fish" and "more" is the same. Thus serving fish last has an auspicious implication that in the future there will always be more. Usually, the whole fish is served since it is polite and respectful to the guest. In recent years, this habit has changed slightly. Sometimes, to make it more convenient for the guest, the bones are removed and the fish is sliced, so only a part of the fish is used.

There are many methods to cook fish. In most Chinese families, fish are often braised, dry fried, deep fried until crispy, steamed, baked, smoked, etc.. The fish itself has no real flavor. No matter what method is used to cook the fish, the fish first should be soaked for a short period. The fish's skin has a certain elasticity to it. When a fish is fried or deep fried, it is easy for the fish to stick to the bottom of the pan. To avoid this, rub some fresh ginger on the bottom of a hot clean pan. Then add the oil. When the oil is hot, the fish can be fried.

煙燻鯧魚

Smoked Fish

材料 >>
白鯧魚1條（約600公克重）、沙拉醬2～3大匙、生菜葉2枚

醃魚料 >>
蔥2支、薑3片、鹽1茶匙、酒1大匙

燻料 >>
白米1/2杯、黃糖（或白糖）1/2杯、紅茶葉1/2杯

做法 >>

1. 將鯧魚切成4片大斜片，用醃魚料拌勻，醃半小時（需常加翻動）。
2. 將魚片擺在盤中，放入滾水鍋上，以大火蒸約8至10分鐘至熟，（盤底要放3支竹筷把魚架起，以便容易蒸熟）。蒸好取出，稍加吹涼。
3. 在一只舊炒鍋內放下燻料，上面放一枚鐵絲網（網上需刷上一層油），將魚排列在網上，蓋好鍋蓋，並用濕毛巾圍住鍋沿，用小火燜燻約10～20分鐘，見顏色已呈茶黃色便可。（在中途需翻面一次）。
4. 用少許油塗亮魚之表面，按魚形排在餐盤中，與沙拉醬同時上桌供食（盤底可墊生菜葉數枚以增美觀）。

Ingredients
1 fish (about 600g.), 2~3 tbsp. mayonnaise, 2 pieces lettuce

Marinades
2 stalks green onion, 3 slices ginger, 1 tsp. salt, 1 tbsp. wine

To smoke fish
1/2 cup rice, 1/2 cup of sugar, 1/2 cup black tea leaves

Procedures

1. Clean the fish and cut it into slices of an appropriate size (about 4 slices). Crush the green onion and ginger, mix with salt and wine; marinate the fish slices for 30 minutes.
2. Arrange the fish on a platter, steam it for about 8 minutes over high heat until done. (If you put three bamboo chopsticks under the fish while steaming, it will get done faster). Remove the fish and let it cools a little.
3. Place the rice, sugar, and black tea leaves in an old iron pan. Place a slightly oiled rack over this and put the fish slices on the rack. Cover and smoke for about 10 minutes over low heat. Turn the fish over and smoke for 5~10 minutes more, smoke until the fish gets brown.
4. Decorate the plate with lettuce leaves. Put the fish attractively on the lettuce and brush with some oil, also put some mayonnaise on the platter as a dipping sauce.

註 此菜也可將魚不蒸而改為用油炸熟後再燻，如把魚切成很薄的片狀時，也可以生燻。
This fish may be fried instead of steamed. This dish may be prepared 1 day before and served cold. It tastes much better when it is cold.

酥炸魚捲
Crisp Fish Curls

材料 >>
白色無骨魚肉400公克、肥豬肉1小塊（煮熟）、荸薺4個、豆腐衣3張、麵粉1大匙（調成糊）、清水1/2大匙（調成糊）、炸油5杯

調味料(A) >>
蔥屑1大匙、薑屑1茶匙、蛋白2大匙、鹽1/3茶匙、酒1茶匙、太白粉2大匙、麻油1茶匙、胡椒粉1/4茶匙

調味料(B) >>
花椒鹽1/2大匙

做法 >>

1. 將魚肉去皮後切成約2.5公分長之粗條狀，放在大碗中，加入肥肉（切絲）及荸薺（剁碎、擠乾水份），再放調味料 (A) 仔細調拌均勻。
2. 將豆腐衣修去尖角成長方形，放入上項1/3量之魚肉料在豆腐衣上，排成一長條，然後由手邊向前捲裹成為一條堅實的筒狀。收口處可用麵粉糊黏住，並向下放在碟中片刻。
3. 在鍋內將炸油燒熱（大約7分熱），放下魚捲用小火炸熟（大約1分多鐘才熟）。
4. 取出後馬上切成小斜段，排入碟內上桌，碟邊備花椒鹽以便沾食。

Ingredients

400g. white meat fish fillets,
80g. pork fat (cooked),
4 water chestnuts,
3 pieces dried tofu wrapper,
1 tbsp. flour,
1/2 tbsp. cold water,
5 cups oil for deep fry

Seasonings (A)

1 tbsp. chopped green onion,
1 tsp. chopped ginger (or 1/4 tsp. ginger powder),
2 tbsp. egg white,
1/3 tsp. salt,
1 tsp. wine,
2 tbsp. cornstarch,
1 tsp. sesame oil,
1/4 black pepper

Seasonings (B)

1/2 tbsp. flavored pepper salt

Procedures

1. Cut the fish into strings (about 2.5cm long). Place into a bowl. Add shredded pork fat, water chestnuts (chopped and squeezed out the excess juice), and seasonings (A). Mix thoroughly.
2. Cut the dried tofu wrapper into a rectangular shape. Place 1/3 of fish mixture on it, roll it into a tight roll, seal the edge with flour paste and then place on a plate (with the edge side face down to seal it tightly).
3. Heat the oil in a pan to about 140ºC. Deep fry the fish roll over high heat for about 1 minute until it is thoroughly done and golden brown.
4. Remove it from oil and cut it into 2cm pieces immediately. Serve hot with flavored pepper salt.

豉汁魚球
Diced Fish with Fermented Black Beans

材料 >>
魚肉400公克、豆豉（切碎）1 1/2大匙、蒜屑1大匙、薑屑1大匙、紅辣椒屑1大匙、蔥粒2大匙、油2杯

醃魚料 >>
鹽1/3茶匙、酒2茶匙、白胡椒粉1/4茶匙

Ingredients
400g. white meat fish fillet,
1 1/2 tbsp. fermented black beans (chopped),
1 tbsp. chopped garlic,
1 tbsp. chopped ginger,
1 tbsp. chopped red pepper,
2 tbsp. chopped green onion,
2 cups oil

To marinate fish
1/3 tsp. salt,
2 tsp. wine,
1/4 tsp. white pepper

Seasonings
3 tbsp. soup stock,
1 tsp. wine,
1/3 tsp. salt,
1/2 tsp. sesame oil,
a pinch of black pepper,
1 tsp. cornstarch

Procedures
1. Cut the fish meat into large slices about 1.5cm thick first, then score the top side lengthwise and crosswise each 1/8 inch deep. Then cut into 2.5cm square pieces. Put in a bowl and marinate for about 30 minutes.
2. Heat oil in a pan. Fry all of the fish over high heat for about 10 seconds. Remove the fish and drain off the oil.
3. Heat the pan again. Add 2 tbsp. oil to stir fry the fermented black beans, garlic, and ginger. After 10 seconds, add the seasoning sauce and fish. Continue stirring gently. Sprinkle the green onion, red pepper, and 1 more table spoon of heated oil on top. Transfer to a serving plate.

 紅辣椒可依個人喜好加入。
If you don't like to eat red hot pepper, don't add it.

綜合調味料 >>

清湯3大匙、酒1茶匙、鹽1/3茶匙、麻油1/2茶匙、胡椒粉少許、太白粉1茶匙

做法 >>

1. 將魚肉整塊先切成1.5公分厚的大片,再在每片上面劃切交叉而細密的淺刀紋,然後全部切成2.5公分四方大小,放在碗裡,用醃魚料拌勻,醃上半小時左右。
2. 將魚片倒進8分熱的油中過油炸熟(約10秒鐘),全部撈出並瀝乾餘油。
3. 起油鍋,用2大匙油炒香豆豉、薑屑及蒜屑,然後倒下綜合調味料煮滾,再將過了油之魚片倒下,輕輕拌鏟均勻,撒下蔥粒及紅辣椒屑,再淋下熱油1大匙,便可起鍋,裝盤後趁熱上桌。

鍋貼魚排
Fried Turreted Fish

材料 >>
白色新鮮魚肉400公克、土司麵包8片、火腿片（3.5公分寬、5公分長）16片、香菜葉1大匙、黑芝麻1/2大匙、炸油6杯、花椒鹽1茶匙、蕃茄醬1大匙

醃魚料 >>
鹽1/3茶匙、酒1/2大匙、太白粉1/2大匙

蛋麵糊料 >>
蛋1個、太白粉3大匙、麵粉5大匙、冷水2大匙

做法 >>

1. 將魚肉用利刀橫面片切成3.5公分寬、5公分長之長方形薄片（約0.6公分厚）。在一只碗內將醃魚料先調勻成糊狀，再加入已切好之魚片，仔細調拌醃上10分鐘左右。
2. 土司麵包先切下硬的黃邊後，每片對切成為2片（每片大小需寬3.5公分、長5公分）。
3. 在一只碗內將蛋打散後，加入麵粉及太白粉與少量的冷水調成蛋麵糊。
4. 將麵包片置砧板上，薄薄的塗上一層上項之麵糊，再蓋上一片魚片；然後在魚片上也塗上一層麵糊，即放上火腿一片；再塗少許蛋糊在火腿上，放一枚香菜葉及少許黑芝麻。即成一個魚排。
5. 將炸油燒成7～8分熱之後，投下全部做好之魚排，應將火腿面向下投入，用小火炸黃（約2分鐘）便可，瀝乾油後排列在盤內，附上少許花椒鹽及蕃茄醬在盤之兩端，上桌蘸用。

Ingredients
400g. fresh fish fillets (sea bass or yellow pike),
8 slices bread,
16 slices ham (3.5 × 5cm),
1 tbsp. parsley leaves,
1/2 tbsp. black sesame seeds,
1 tsp. flavored pepper salt,
1 tbsp. ketchup,
6 cups oil for deep fry

To marinate fish
1/3 tsp. salt,
1/2 tbsp. wine,
1/2 tbsp. cornstarch

To make flour paste
1 egg,
3 tbsp. cornstarch,
5 tbsp. flour,
2 tbsp. cold water

Procedures

1 After removing the skin and bones, cut the fish diagonally into 16 slices with 3.5cm wide, 5cm long, 0.6cm thick. Place in a large bowl and mix with the marinades. Stay for about 10 minutes..

2 Remove the hard crust from each slice of bread. Then cut into 3.5cm wide, and 5cm long pieces.

3 Make the flour paste with the beaten egg, flour, cornstarch, and cold water.

4 Place sliced bread on a board. Rub some flour paste on top. Then place 1 slice of fish meat and rub some flour paste on top again. Put 1 slice of ham over it. Decorate the top of the ham with 1 parsley leaf and some black sesame seeds (rub some flour batter on ham first).

5 Heat oil in a frying pan about 140~150ºC. Drop the fish sandwich into oil (decorated side down). Fry until golden brown over low heat (about 2 minutes) . Remove and drain. Pat on a platter. Serve with flavored pepper salt and ketchup.

 花椒鹽的做法在培梅食譜第一冊第19頁，魚排也可用平底鍋，使用少量的油煎熟，而不必炸。

The recipe for flavored pepper salt can be found on p.19 of Pei Mei's Chinese Cook Book Vol. I. The dish can also be fried with less oil in a flat pan.

紅燒划水
Braised Fish Tails in Brown Sauce

材料 >>
草魚尾1段（約15公分長）（或其他淡水大型魚之魚尾均可）、太白粉2茶匙、油6大匙、蔥1支、薑2片、青蒜絲1/2杯

醃魚料 >>
醬油4大匙、胡椒粉少許

調味料 >>
酒1/2大匙、糖1大匙、醬色1茶匙、清湯（或水）1杯、麻油1茶匙

做法 >>

1. 將魚尾刮洗乾淨後，斬除少許尾鰭之尖梢，再直刀切成5塊（約0.8公分寬之直條狀）全部放在盆中用醬油和胡椒粉拌醃5分鐘左右。

2. 在碟中，將2茶匙太白粉加入2大匙冷水調開備用。

3. 在炒鍋內燒熱5大匙油後，放下蔥、薑煎黃，（隨即取出不要）再將已醃好之魚塊兩面均沾上太白粉水，逐一放下油鍋中，兩面輕輕煎過（每面僅煎3秒鐘）。

4. 待全部煎過之後，在鍋內排列整齊，淋下酒，並加入醃魚所剩下之醬油汁，再加糖與醬色及清湯，蓋上鍋蓋，用中火煮約5分鐘，至魚肉熟透已可離骨為止。

5. 用手提起鍋子搖轉一下，並淋下沾魚所剩之濕太白粉水，使汁黏稠。澆上1大匙熱油，並撒下切成斜細絲之青蒜、淋下少許麻油，便可端起鍋子、輕輕推滑在菜盤中，撒少許胡椒粉後端上桌。（推入盤中後仍需保持5條原排形狀）

Ingredients

1 fresh water fish tail (about 15cm long),
2 tsp. cornstarch (add 1 tbsp. water),
2 slices ginger,
6 tbsp. oil, 1 stalk green onion,
1/2 cup shredded green garlic or green onion

To marinate fish

4 tbsp. soy sauce,
1/4 tsp. black pepper

Seasonings

1/2 tbsp. wine,
1 tbsp. sugar,
1 tsp. food coloring (dark brown),
1 cup soup stock or water,
1 tsp. sesame oil

Procedures

1. Scale and clean the fish tail and cut off part of the tail fin; then cut it into 5 pieces about 0.8 cm wide and then marinate for 5 minutes.
2. Mix 2 tsp. cornstarch and 2 tbsp. water in a dish for later use.
3. Heat 5 tbsp. oil in a frying pan. Fry the green onion and ginger for a few seconds until dark, then discard it. Coat the fish's tail with the above cornstarch paste. Place into the frying pan. Fry each side for 3 seconds.
4. Arrange all fish tail in one direction, sprinkle wine, the remaining portion of the soy sauce, sugar, food coloring and soup stock into the pan. Covered and cook for about 5 minutes over low heat until the fish is tender and done.
5. Lift the pan up and shake it gently in, pour in the remaining portion of the cornstarch paste (that was used to coat the fish tail) to thicken the sauce. Then sprinkle with 1 tbsp. heated oil, shredded green garlic and sesame oil. Gently push the fish onto a platter for immediate serving. (you may sprinkle some black pepper on first at last).

紅燒鰻魚

Braised Eel with Brown Sauce

材料 >>
河鰻600公克、冬筍2支、香菇5個、白果1/2杯、蔥屑1大匙、薑屑1大匙、肥肉片1大匙、油4大匙、網油1張、青蒜絲（或蔥絲）2大匙

調味料(A)
酒1大匙、醬油3大匙、糖1大匙、醬色1茶匙、水1 1/2杯

調味料(B)
太白粉水2茶匙、鎮江醋1/2大匙、麻油1/2大匙

做法 >>

1. 將已殺好之鰻魚整條投入8分滾之開水中（即8杯水煮滾之後加入一杯冷水）燙約3秒鐘。撈出後刷淨表皮上白色黏液，斬切成約3.5公分長之小段。
2. 筍切滾刀塊備用；白果用水沖洗數次，瀝乾。
3. 起油鍋，用4大匙油炒肥肉，再爆香蔥、薑屑，放下香菇和筍塊同炒，並加入調味料(A)（除醋與麻油外）。將鰻魚段和白果放下排好，再將網油覆蓋在上面包住魚塊，以小火煮約20分鐘左右，至湯汁剩下半杯為止。
4. 慢慢淋下太白粉水勾芡，要提起鍋子搖動，使湯汁黏稠。淋下醋及麻油，便將網油揭開，撒下青蒜絲、輕輕推入菜盤內即成。

Ingredients
600g. eel,
2 bamboo shoots,
5 black mushrooms (soaked),
1/2 cup ginkgo,
1 tbsp. chopped green onion,
1 tbsp. chopped ginger,
1 tbsp. diced pork fat,
4 tbsp. oil,
1 piece net lard (optional),
2 tbsp. shredded green garlic or green onion

Seasonings A
1 tbsp. wine,
3 tbsp. soy sauce,
1 tbsp. sugar,
1 tsp. dark brown food coloring (optional),
1 1/2 cups water

Seasonings B
2 tsp. cornstarch paste,
1/2 tbsp. brown vinegar,
1/2 tbsp. sesame oil

Procedures

1. Place cleaned eel into almost boiling water (by adding 1 cup of cold water into 8 cups of boiling water) and blanch for only 3 seconds. Lift eel out and brush off excess viscous film. Cut into 3.5 cm sections.
2. Cut the bamboo shoots to pieces or slices. Rinse gingko for several times, drain.
3. Heat 4 tbsp. oil in a pan to stir fry pork fat, stir in the green onion, ginger and finally the mushrooms and bamboo shoots. Add the seasonings (A) and arrange the eel and ginkgo in, cover with the net lard over it. Cook over low heat for about 20 minutes until the water is reduced to 1/2 cup.
4. Thicken the water with cornstarch paste, add vinegar and sesame oil at last, remove the net lard. Sprinkle shredded green garlic over. Gently pour it into a large platter, serve immediately.

咖哩魚片
Sliced Fish with Curry Sauce

材料 >>
新鮮白色魚肉300公克、洋蔥丁1/2杯、香菇丁1/4杯、青豆2大匙、太白粉1/2杯、炸油5杯、咖哩粉1 1/2大匙

醃魚料 >>
蛋白1大匙、太白粉1大匙、鹽1/4茶匙、胡椒粉少許

綜合調味料 >>
糖1大匙、水5大匙、酒1/2大匙、鹽1/3茶匙、蕃茄醬1大匙、太白粉1茶匙、麻油少許

做法 >>
1. 將魚去皮除骨後，順紋切成約3.5公分長，5公分寬之長方形薄片。在碗中先打散蛋白，再加入太白粉及鹽調勻成糊狀，再加入已切好之魚片仔細調拌，醃約半小時。
2. 將魚片在乾太白粉中（或麵粉）兩面沾敷。全部沾好後放置3分鐘，投入已燒熱之炸油中炸黃（大火炸約1分鐘），撈出魚片、將油倒出。
3. 另在鍋中燒熱2大匙油，先炒洋蔥丁，再放咖哩粉炒香，繼續放入冬菇丁同炒數下，隨後將綜合調味料傾入，以大火煮滾（需不停加以攪動、拌勻）。
4. 放下青豆即熄火，再將魚片落鍋，略加拌合均勻，即可裝盤。

Ingredients
300g. fish fillet, 1/2 tbsp. diced onion, 1/4 cup diced black mushroom, 2 tbsp. green peas, 1/2 cup cornstarch, 5 cups oil for deep fry, 1 1/2 tbsp. curry powder

To marinate fish
1 tbsp. egg white, 1 tbsp. cornstarch, 1/4 tsp. salt, a pinch of black pepper

Seasonings
1 tbsp. sugar, 5 tbsp. water, 1/2 tbsp. wine, 1/3 tsp. salt, 1 tbsp. ketchup, 1 tsp. cornstarch, 1 tsp. sesame oil

Procedures
1. Rinse and pat dry the fish. Cut it into 3.5cm wide, 5cm long thin slices. Mix the marinades evenly first, and then add the fish slices in, marinate for about half an hour.
2. Coat the fish slices with cornstarch and then deep fry in hot oil for about 1 minute until it becomes brown and crispy. Remove it and drain off the oil.
3. Heat 3 tbsp. oil in a frying pan to stir fry the diced onions and curry. Then add black mushroom in, stir fry until fragrant. Pour the mixed seasoning sauce in. Stir briskly until it thickened.
4. Add green peas. Turn off the heat and add the fried fish. Mix until blended. Serve immediately.

註 此菜中的魚片亦可不用沾太白粉而過油的方法（即醃後直接泡油致熟法）。沾粉再炸的魚片食時較酥脆，過油的則滑嫩。

If you like, you can deep fry the fish without coating it with cornstarch. The cornstarch makes the fish crispier.

豆豉辣椒蒸魚

Steamed Fish with Fermented Black Beans and Hot Pepper

材料 >>
活草魚（或鯉魚）1條（約600公克重）、乾豆豉2大匙、薑屑1大匙、紅辣椒屑1大匙、熟火腿絲1大匙、蔥粒1大匙、熱油2大匙

調味料 >>
鹽1茶匙、酒1大匙、醬油1大匙

做法 >>

1. 將魚刮洗乾淨，由腹部從頭到尾全部劃開、使魚成為背部仍相連之一大片，再在魚肉較厚處直切兩刀刀口，並斬斷數處大骨，然後撒上 1/2 茶匙鹽及酒抹勻，醃 10 分鐘。
2. 豆豉洗過，放在碗中，加入切成細末之火腿、薑、紅辣椒與另外半茶匙鹽和 1 大匙醬油，調拌均勻。
3. 將魚放在長形餐盤內（魚背向上），在面上平均撒下前項混拌之材料（如有網油，則把網油覆蓋上去，將整條魚包裹起來更好）。
4. 待蒸鍋中之水已沸滾之後，放進整盤魚，用大火蒸約 10 分鐘（見魚眼突出而泛白即是已熟）。
5. 將魚端出後，撒下蔥粒並淋下燒滾之熱油 2 大匙，趁熱上桌供食，其味鮮美無比，係湖南名菜之一。

Ingredients

1 live fish (carp or any fresh water fish, about 600 g.),
2 tbsp. dried fermented black beans,
1 tbsp. chopped ginger,
1 tbsp. chopped red pepper,
1 tbsp. shredded ham,
1 tbsp. chopped green onion,
2 tbsp. oil

Seasonings

1 tbsp. salt,
1 tbsp. wine,
1 tbsp. soy sauce

Procedures

1. Scale and clean the fish. Split it lengthwise from gills down without cutting thorough the back. Chop the large bones into sections, and then rub 1/2 tsp. salt and wine over fish, marinate for a few minutes.
2. Rinse the fermented black beans. Remove the seeds from the pepper and then chop it. Mix the beans and red pepper with 1/2 tsp. salt, soy sauce, ham, and ginger in a small bowl.
3. Put the fish on a platter (the fish's back up). Sprinkle the No. 2 mixture on the fish.
4. Steam the fish over high heat for about 10 minutes until the fish's eyes become white and pop out.
5. Remove the fish platter from the steamer. Sprinkle chopped green onion and 2 tbsp. heated oil over the fish. Serve hot. This is a very famous Hunan dish.

註 If you cover the fish just before steaming with a large sheet of net lard, it will taste better.

材料 >>
白色魚肉300公克、豆腐衣4張、蔥屑1大匙、薑屑1茶匙、蒜屑1大匙、炸油6杯

醃魚料 >>
蛋白1大匙、鹽1/3茶匙、酒1茶匙、麻油1茶匙、胡椒粉1/4茶匙、蔥屑1/2大匙、薑汁1/2茶匙

綜合調味料 >>
蕃茄醬2大匙、糖3大匙、醋2大匙、清水4大匙、鹽1/3茶匙、太白粉2茶匙、麻油1茶匙

做法 >>
1. 將魚肉切成如大姆指甲般大小之片狀，放在碗裡，加入醃魚料先拌勻，然後再加入蔥屑、薑汁繼續調拌好。
2. 將每張豆腐衣平均切成4個尖角的小張後，分別用來包裹上項材料（每張放1大匙），使成為長方形小包（封口處用少許調水之麵粉糊黏住）。
3. 在鍋內將炸油燒到8成熱後，放下全部魚捲，用小火炸2分鐘左右至成為金黃色止。撈出，排列在盤內。
4. 另外燒熱1大匙油炒香蒜及薑屑，倒下綜合調味料，用大火煮滾，再淋下1大匙熱油，撒下蔥屑，熄火，全部澆到盤中魚捲上，趁熱送席。

Ingredients
300g. fish fillet (sea bass or yellow pike), 4 pieces dried tofu wrapper, 6 cups oil for deep fry, 1 tbsp. chopped green onion, 1 tsp. chopped ginger, 1 tbsp. chopped garlic

To marinate fish
1 tbsp. egg white, 1/3 tsp. salt, 1 tsp.wine, 1 tsp. sesame oil, 1/4 tsp. black pepper, 1/2 tbsp. chopped green onion, 1/2 tsp. ginger juice

Seasonings
2 tbsp. ketchup, 3 tbsp. sugar, 2 tbsp. vinegar, 4 tbsp. cold water, 1/3 tsp. salt, 2 tsp. cornstarch, 1 tsp. sesame oil

Procedures
1. Cut the fish meat into thin slices. Place into a bowl. Mix thoroughly with marinades, then add chopped green onion and ginger. Blend again.
2. Cut each piece of tofu wrapper into 4 triangles. Put 1 tbsp. of the fish mixture on the wrapper. Then fold up the corners to make a package. Seal with some flour paste.
3. Deep fry all the fish packages in hot oil for about 2 minutes until golden. Remove to a platter.
4. Heat another 2 tbsp. oil in the pan. Stir fry chopped garlic and ginger. Then add the seasoning sauce. Bring to a boil. Splash 1 tbsp. heated oil into the sauce. Then sprinkle chopped green onion in. Turn off the heat. Pour this sauce over the fish rolls. Serve.

糖醋魚捲
Fish Rolls with Sweet and Sour Sauce

註
1. 如無豆腐衣可用春捲皮或蛋皮代替之。
2. 可用洋蔥丁，胡蘿蔔丁與青豆各少許代替蔥屑、薑屑、蒜屑（煮在糖醋汁之配料）。

1. Instead of dried tofu wrapper, egg sheet or egg roll wrapper may be used.
2. You may use diced onion, carrot and green peas instead of the chopped green onion, ginger and garlic for the seasoning sauce ingredients.

白汁燴全魚
Steamed Fish with Cream Sauce

材料 >>
新鮮魚1條（約600公克重）、油3大匙、蔥1支、薑2片、清湯1杯、筍片（1公分四方）3大匙、洋菇片3大匙、火腿片（1公分四方）2大匙、青豆2大匙

醃魚料 >>
鹽2/3茶匙、酒1大匙、蔥2支、薑3片

調味料 >>
鹽1/3茶匙、胡椒粉少許、麻油1/2茶匙、太白粉水1/2大匙、蛋白1個、鮮奶油或奶水2大匙

做法 >>

1. 將魚身兩面切入交叉斜刀紋後，用醃魚料（蔥、薑需拍碎）反覆擦抹魚身，並放置10分鐘。
2. 撿棄蔥、薑後，將魚平放在碟子上（魚身下面需橫架兩支竹筷），然後移進水已沸滾之蒸鍋中，用大火蒸約10～12分鐘（見魚之眼珠已變白而突出為止），將魚放到大餐盤內。將蒸出之魚汁倒棄。
3. 在炒鍋內燒熱2大匙油後，放下蔥支和薑片，炸至焦黃後撈出、然後加入清湯，放下筍片、洋菇片、火腿片，再煮一滾，並放鹽、胡椒粉和麻油調味，然後用太白粉水勾芡（不可太黏）。
4. 將火改小，慢慢淋下打散之蛋白（攪動蛋汁、使其成為細絲狀），最後將牛奶水加入，拌攪均勻即可熄火，全部澆到魚身上。

Ingredients

1 whole fish (about 600g.),
3 tbsp. oil,
1 stalk green onion,
2 slices ginger,
1 cup soup stock,
3 tbsp. diced bamboo shoot (1cm square),
3 tbsp. sliced mushrooms,
2 tbsp. diced ham (1cm square),
2 tbsp. green peas

To smoke fish

2/3 tsp. salt,
1 tbsp. wine,
2 stalks green onion,
3 slices ginger

Seasonings

1/3 tsp. salt,
1/4 tsp. pepper,
1/2 tsp. sesame oil,
1/2 tbsp. cornstarch paste,
2 tbsp. egg white,
2 tbsp. condensed milk or cream

Procedures

1. Score the fish on each side with crisscross diagonals. Cut 2.5cm apart and almost to the large bone. Marinate with salt, wine, green onion and ginger. Let it stand for about 10 minutes.
2. Place fish on 2 crossed chopsticks on a plate so that the bottom of the fish can get done quickly. Steam the fish for 10~12 minutes. When the fish's eyes pop out and turn white, it is done. Transfer it to a serving platter. Remove the chopsticks, and discard the liquid from steamed fish.
3. Heat 2 tbsp. oil in a fry pan. Fry the green onion and ginger until golden brown. Remove and discard it. Add the soup stock, the sliced bamboo shoots, mushrooms, hams and green peas. Bring to a boil. Season with salt, pepper and sesame oil. Thicken with cornstarch paste.
4. Reduce the heat to low. Add the beaten egg white carefully and stir until blende. Finally, add the milk or cream. Turn off the heat. Pour all of the sauce over the fish. Serve.

海 鮮 篇

有關蝦與海鮮類

蝦之種類及名稱繁多,可按形狀之大、小、長、短分為大蝦、中蝦、小蝦,而又按菜式之需要決定採用何種大小之蝦。一般乾燒或乾煎(帶殼用)需購買小型之大蝦(又叫明蝦)或是大一點的中蝦。如係炒蝦仁,則用小蝦或小型的中蝦皆可。如做蝦丸之類,需將蝦肉剁碎成泥狀者,可購買小蝦(因價格較低廉)。由於蝦肉缺少脂肪成份,故用剁爛之蝦肉做菜時需加放20％絞爛之肥豬肉同拌,才會鬆香可口。用蝦烹調之菜色,切忌調味太重,反而會減少了其原本之鮮美。

通常中國菜單上所列之海鮮類係指"魚"以外,在海中所產之各種材料,包括蝦在內,其他如:蟹、蠔、螺、魷魚、墨魚、干貝、海參、鮑魚、蛤蜊等均屬味道鮮美人人愛吃的,且營養價值很高之海鮮。

About Shrimp and Seafood

There are many different sizes of shrimp. Usually they are divided into two main classes: prawns (about 4 to 6 inches long) and shrimp (about 1 1/2 inches long). In addition, there are others whose sizes do not fit in the above mentioned classes. The method of cooking these shrimps depends on their size. Prawns are often braised, stewed or dried fried, while small shrimp are frequently stir fried or deep fried, If shrimp balls are made, the shrimp must be chopped very fine, so small shrimp may be used (they are cheaper). Due to the lack of fat content in shrimp, 20% (of the shrimp) minced pork fat must be added and mixed well with the shrimp.

The Chinese word seafood includes everything except fish. Therefore, seafood includes: shrimp, crab, oysters, conch meat, cuttlefish, squid, scallops, sea cucumbers, abalone, clams, etc. All of them are full of nutrition, and taste delicious.

子母蝦
Baby and Mother Shrimps

材料 >>
蝦仁200公克、蔥粒1大匙、薑片（花片）10小片、中型明蝦8隻、蔥屑2大匙、薑屑1大匙、蕃茄醬3大匙、太白粉水1/2大匙、青菜300公克

醃蝦仁料 >>
蛋白1大匙、太白粉2茶匙

調味料(A) >>
酒1大匙、鹽1/3茶匙、麻油1/2茶匙

調味料(B) >>
酒1大匙、清湯2/3杯、糖1/2大匙、鹽2/3茶匙

做法 >>
1. 蝦仁沖洗過之後擦乾，用調勻之醃蝦料拌醃約半小時。
2. 在鍋內燒熱1杯油後，將蝦仁過油炸熟（約10秒鐘），撈出瀝乾。油也倒出，只留下1大匙，用來炒香蔥粒及薑片，並落蝦仁回鍋，淋下調味料(A)炒勻即可盛在圓盤之中央。
3. 明蝦用剪刀剪開背殼，抽出砂腸，再剪下蝦頭之前半段及尾部之尖角，蝦腳也全部剪下。用刀在背部切入很深之刀口。
4. 燒熱3大匙油，將蝦落鍋煎紅，加入調味料(B)煮約2分鐘至熟，全部倒入碗內（連汁）。
5. 另用油2大匙炒香蔥屑及薑屑，並加入蕃茄醬炒紅，然後將上項蝦連汁全部倒入鍋內再煮一滾，淋下太白粉水使汁黏稠。全部和蝦仁與青菜一起排盤上桌。

Ingredients
200g. shelled shrimp,
1 tbsp. chopped green onion,
10 slices ginger, 8 prawns,
2 tbsp. chopped green onion,
1 tbsp. chopped ginger,
3 tbsp. ketchup,
1/2 tbsp. cornstarch paste,
300g. green vegetables

To marinate shrimp
1 tbsp. egg white,
2 tsp. cornstarch

Procedures
1. Rinse the shrimp and then pat it dry with paper towel. Marinate for half an hour.
2. Heat 1 cup of oil to fry the shrimp for about 10 seconds until done. Remove the shrimp and pour out the oil. Heat 1 tbsp. oil to stir fry the green onion and ginger for a few seconds, add the shrimp and the seasonings (A). Stir thoroughly. Place in the center of a platter.
3. Cut the back shell of the prawns through with a scissors. Cut off the sharp part of head, the tail's needle, and the feet. Cut a deep score in the prawn's back with a knife.
4. Heat 3 tbsp. oil to fry the prawns until they turn red (both sides). Add seasonings (B), cook for 2 minutes until done. Remove the prawns and sauce to a bowl.
5. Heat another 2 tbsp. oil to stir fry the green onion, ginger, and ketchup. Stir fry until the oil turns red. Add the prawns and sauce. Bring to a boil and then thicken with cornstarch paste. Arrange on the platter with shrimp and cooked vegetable. Serve.

Seasonings (A)
1 tbsp. wine,
1/3 tsp. salt,
1/2 tsp. sesame oil

Seasonings (B)
1 tbsp. wine,
2/3 cup soup stock,
1/2 tbsp. sugar,
2/3 tsp. salt

海鮮篇
培梅食譜 II

乾燒蝦碌
Sautéed Prawn with Tomato Sauce

材料 >>
中型明蝦6隻（約600公克重）、洋蔥（切絲）2杯、太白粉水1/2大匙

綜合調味料 >>
蕃茄醬3大匙、酒1大匙、辣醬油2大匙、糖1大匙、鹽1/2茶匙、清水1/2杯、胡椒粉少許、麻油數滴

做法 >>
1. 明蝦先剪除頭尖部份，再剪去尾尖部份與腳，並剪開背部，抽出腸砂，然後洗淨、瀝乾，切成兩段。
2. 將洋蔥絲用2大匙油炒熟至軟，加鹽1/4茶匙調味後，盛入盤中。
3. 再燒熱3大匙油，放下全部明蝦，將鍋傾斜、轉動，使每隻明蝦均能被油煎到，待一面呈紅色後便翻轉一面再煎（用小火），至明蝦全部煎紅而熟後，淋下酒1大匙即可全部盛出。
4. 在原炒鍋內另燒熱2大匙油，傾入蕃茄醬炒紅，再倒下其餘之綜合調味料，待煮滾後將明蝦傾入鍋內，再煮1分鐘，淋下太白粉水勾芡（提起鍋子搖轉、使汁黏稠），即可倒在盤中之洋蔥上送席。

Ingredients
6 fresh prawns (about 600g.),
2 cups shredded onion,
1/2 tbsp. cornstarch paste

Seasonings
3 tbsp. ketchup,
1 tbsp. wine,
2 tbsp. worcestershire sauce,
1 tbsp. sugar,
1/2 tsp. salt,
1/2 cup water,
1/4 tsp. black pepper,
1/4 tsp. sesame oil

Procedures
1. Cut off the prawn's head, sharp tail, and feet. Then cut each prawn down the back and de-vein it. Rinse the prawns, drain and dry it, then cut each prawn into two sections.
2. Stir fry the shredded onion with 2 tbsp. oil until soft. Season with 1/2 tsp. salt. Remove to a platter.
3. Heat 3 tbsp. oil to fry the prawns, gently shake the pan so that each prawn will be cooked evenly. When they turn red, turn them over and fry the other side until completely done. Sprinkle in 1 tbsp. wine. Then remove.
4. Heat another 2 tbsp. oil in the same pan. Add the ketchup and all the other seasoning sauce, bring to a boil. Then put the fried prawns into the sauce. Cook for 1 minute. Thicken with cornstarch paste. Sprinkle 1 tbsp. heated oil. Place over the fried onions and serve.

西炸小蝦排
Deep-fried Shrimp Cutlets

材料 >>

蝦仁48隻、蔥2支、薑3片、雞蛋2個、麵粉1/2杯、麵包粉1杯、牙籤12支、炸油6杯

調味料 >>

酒1/2大匙、鹽1/3茶匙、胡椒粉少許

做法 >>

1. 將蝦仁洗淨，拭乾水份，放在碗內，加入拍碎之蔥、薑和調味料拌醃約10分鐘左右。
2. 用一支牙籤穿上先排列好之4隻蝦仁成為一串，並用手指略為壓平，逐個做好後，每排先沾上一層乾麵粉，再在碗中打散之蛋汁中沾裹一下，最後敷滿麵包粉，用手指壓實後備炸。
3. 將炸油在鍋內燒至8成熱後，投下蝦排（由鍋邊向油中滑落，此時需將牙籤迅速抽出），用小火炸至兩面均呈金黃色而蝦仁已熟為止。全部撈出，趁熱排列在餐盤中，附上花椒鹽及蕃茄醬在盤邊即可上桌供食。

Ingredients

48 pieces small shrimp (shelled),
2 stalks green onion,
3 slices ginger,
2 eggs,
1/2 cup flour,
1 cup bread crumbs,
12 pieces tooth pick,
6 cups oil for deep fry

Seasonings

1/2 tbsp. wine,
1/2 tsp. salt,
1/4 tsp. black pepper

Procedures

1. Rinse the shrimp and pat it dry. Add the chopped green onion, ginger and marinades to marinate shrimp for about 10 minutes.
2. Put 4 pieces of shrimp on a tooth pick. Coyer them with dry flour. Then dip them in the beaten eggs and coat them with bread crumbs at last.
3. Heat the oil in a pan to 160°C to deep fry the shrimps, remove the tooth pick when you slip the shrimp to the oil. Deep fry over medium heat until they become golden brown. Drain and arrange it on a plate, serve with peppercorn salt or ketchup.

蛋黃蝦
Prawns and Egg Yolk Sandwiches

材料 >>
中型明蝦4隻（約500公克重）、土司麵包4片、肥肉1塊（約100公克）、鹹蛋黃4個、白芝麻1/2大匙、炸油5杯

蛋麵糊 >>
蛋1個、麵粉3大匙、太白粉3大匙、水2大匙

調味料 >>
鹽1/4茶匙、酒1茶匙

做法 >>
1. 將蝦摘除蝦頭，並剝去蝦殼（留下蝦尾不剝），抽出砂腸後，將每隻蝦從背部剖開、使成為一大片平面狀，用調味料拌醃約10分鐘左右。
2. 蛋在小碗內打散，加麵粉等調成蛋麵糊；鹹蛋黃略為壓扁一些備用。
3. 土司麵包先切除四週黃邊後，每片再橫切成兩片；肥肉先在冰箱中冰硬、切成8片與土司麵包相同大小之薄片。
4. 將土司麵包一片平擺在板上，塗上一層蛋麵糊、放上一片肥肉，又塗上一層蛋麵糊，然後將整個鹹蛋黃擺上，再將明蝦片蓋到鹹蛋黃上，再塗上一層蛋麵糊在蝦片上，然後再放上一片肥肉，最後又塗上一層麵糊，並撒上少許白芝麻。
5. 燒熱炸油，將做好的蛋黃蝦下鍋，用小火炸熟（約3分鐘）。撈出之後，每隻直面對半切開，切面向上排入盤內便可。

Procedures
1. Remove the head from the prawn and peel the shell off except for the tail shell; de-vein it. Split each prawn lengthwise from the back, but don't sever it, so the prawn is a large and flat piece. Marinate with salt and wine for about 10 minutes.
2. In a small bowl, beat the egg to prepare the flour paste. Press the salty egg yolk gently to make it flat
3. Remove the crust from the sliced bread. Cut each slice into 2 thin pieces. Cut the pork fat (frozen it first) into 8 paper thin slices-the same size as the bread.
4. Spread some flour paste on each piece of bread. Put 1 slice of pork fat on the bread and then spread some paste over the pork fat. Then put one egg yolk on the pork fat and cover the egg yolk with 1 prawn. Spread some paste over the prawn and put 1 slice of pork fat on top again. At last, spread some paste over the pork fat and sprinkle some sesame seeds on top.
5. Heat the oil in a pan. Deep fry the sandwich over low heat for about 3 minutes until done and golden brown. Remove and cut each sandwich lengthwise into two pieces. Arrange on the platter (cut side up) and serve.

Ingredients
4 prawns (about 500g.),
4 slices bread,
1 piece pork fat (about 100g.),
4 salted duck egg yolks (or cooked egg yolks),
1/2 tbsp. white sesame seeds,
5 cups oil for deep fry

Flour paste
1 egg,
3 tbsp. flour,
3 tbsp. cornstarch,
2 tbsp. water

Seasonings
1/4 tsp. salt,
1 tsp. wine

紫菜蝦捲
Minced Shrimp Rolls

材料 >>
蝦仁250公克、絞肥肉80公克、紫菜（海苔）3大張、炸油5杯、香菜1撮

拌蝦料 >>
蔥薑水2大匙、酒1/2大匙、鹽1/3茶匙、太白粉1大匙、蛋白半個（約1大匙）

做法 >>

1. 蝦仁用刀面壓碎之後，加入肥肉一起仔細再剁爛成為泥狀。裝在大碗內，加入拌蝦料，再仔細而順著同一方向攪拌成膠狀。
2. 紫菜每張分切成6小張，在每張上面靠手邊的地方，放下1/2大匙的蝦肉，然後捲成筒狀，並捏擠蝦肉使成為粗細平均的紫菜捲，封口處用蝦肉少許沾住（兩端應露出少許蝦肉以增美觀）
3. 用約120°C溫熱的油將蝦捲全部以小火炸熟（約2分鐘）。撈出後裝碟內，飾以香菜即可。

Ingredients

250g. small shrimp (shelled),
80g. ground pork fat,
3 pieces sea weed,
5 cups oil for deep fry,
a little of parsley

Seasonings

2 tbsp. green onion and ginger juice,
1/2 tbsp. wine,
1/3 tsp. salt,
1 tbsp. cornstarch,
1 tbsp. egg white

Procedures

1. Pound the shrimp with the back of a knife, Add the pork fat and chop them finely. Put in a bowl. Add the green onion and ginger juice, wine, salt, cornstarch, and egg white. The stir well in one general drection until sticky.
2. Cut each piece of sea weed into six pieces. Place 1/2 tbsp. shrimp mixture on sea weed (near the edge), roll it into a tight roll. Use a little shrimp mixture to seal the edge. (To make it looks nice, the shrimp mixture should come out a little from the two edges).
3. Heat oil to 120°C. To deep fry the shrimp rolls over medium low heat for about 2 minutes until they are thoroughly done. Remove and arrange on a platter. Garnish with some parsley. Serve.

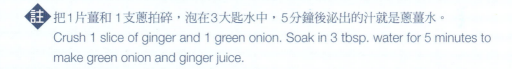

把1片薑和1支蔥拍碎，泡在3大匙水中，5分鐘後泌出的汁就是蔥薑水。
Crush 1 slice of ginger and 1 green onion. Soak in 3 tbsp. water for 5 minutes to make green onion and ginger juice.

醋溜明蝦片
Deep-fried Prawns with Sour Sauce

材料 >>
明蝦6隻（或大型中蝦12隻）、太白粉1/2杯、大蒜片2大匙、乾木耳2大匙、毛豆（或青豆）2大匙、胡蘿蔔片（煮熟）2大匙、炸油5杯

醃蝦用 >>
蛋白2大匙、鹽1/3茶匙、太白粉1大匙

綜合調味料 >>
鎮江醋（或白醋）3大匙、糖3大匙、清湯或水6大匙、鹽1/4茶匙、太白粉2茶匙、麻油1/4茶匙

做法 >>

1. 明蝦摘除蝦頭，並剝去外殼（留下尾殼），抽出砂腸後略沖洗一下，拭乾水份。將每隻由背部下刀，剖開成兩半，然後再直刀切成兩段，全部切好，放在大碗內，用醃蝦料拌勻，醃約半小時左右，再在每片蝦上沾上太白粉備炸。
2. 大蒜去皮、切片；木耳泡發後去蒂、撕成小塊；毛豆燙熟備用。
3. 將綜合調味料先調好備用。
4. 炸油燒熱，放入蝦片、大火炸熟（約30秒鐘），瀝出蝦後，油倒出。
5. 另在鍋內燒熱2大匙油，先炒蒜片，再放入木耳、胡蘿蔔片和毛豆同炒，隨後倒下綜合調味料煮滾。見汁變稠時，即可熄火、將蝦片落鍋，快速拌勻即裝盤。

Ingredients
6 prawns or 12 large shrimp,
1/2 cup cornstarch (for coating),
2 tbsp. garlic slices,
2 tbsp. black fungus,
2 tbsp. fresh soy beans or green peas,
2 tbsp. sliced carrot (cooked),
5 cups oil for deep fry

To marinate prawns
2 tbsp. egg white,
1/3 tsp. salt,
1 tbsp. cornstarch

Seasonings
3 tbsp. brown vinegar,
3 tbsp. sugar,
6 tbsp. soup stock or water,
1/4 tsp. salt,
2 tsp. cornstarch,
1/4 tsp. sesame oil

Procedures
1. Remove the head and the shell (but keep the tail's shell), also de-vein the prawns. Rinse and pat it dry. Split each prawn lengthwise into 2 pieces, then cut crosswise into two pieces (one piece will have a tail and the other will not). Place in a bowl; mix with marinades; stay for about 1/2 hour. Coat each piece of prawn with cornstarch lightly.
2. Slice the garlic. After softening the fungus, remove the stems and tear it into small pieces. Cook the soy bean until done.
3. Prepare the seasoning sauce in a bowl.
4. Heat the oil to deep fry the prawns over high heat for about 30 seconds until done. Remove the prawns and drain off the oil.
5. Reheat 2 tbsp. oil in the same pan. Stir fry the garlic for a few seconds; add the fungus, carrot, and soy beans. Stir for a few seconds again. Pour in the seasoning sauce and bring to a boil. Turn off the heat and put the fried prawns into the sauce. Mix well; remove to a platter and serve.

大燴鮑片

Abalone with Assorted Vegetables

材料 >>
鮑魚（罐頭）1罐、小青江菜10支、玉米筍8支、洋菇10粒、罐頭蘆筍10支、熟鵪鶉蛋10個、清湯2杯

調味料 >>
醬油1大匙、鹽1/2茶匙、太白粉水1 1/2大匙

Ingredients
1 can abalone,
10 green cabbages (2" long),
8 baby corns,
10 mushrooms,
10 asparagus tips (3" long),
10 cooked quail eggs,
2 cups soup stock

Seasonings
1 tbsp. soy sauce,
1/2 tsp. salt,
1 1/2 tbsp. cornstarch paste

Procedures
1. Remove the abalone from the can; remove the outer edge of the abalone and then slice It into thin round slices.
2. Remove the outer leaves from the green cabbages. Trim it into 2 inches long. Blanch for 1/2 minute. Remove and plunge into cold water imarinateediately until cool. Then squeeze dry. Cut the baby corn into diagonal shape, also boil it for a while, remove and drain.
3. Cut off the mushroom stems and slice it into round slices. Cut the asparagus into two pieces.
4. Heat 2 tbsp. oil to stir fry the mushrooms. Add the soup stock and 1/2 cup of abalone soup from the can. Season with salt and soy sauce. When it boils, add the quail eggs, baby corn, and green cabbages. Bring to a boil. Thicken with the cornstarch paste.
5. Add the asparagus. When it boils again, remove all of the ingredients and half of the soup to the platter. Then add the abalone to the soup; bring to a boil again. Pour over the vegetables and serve.

做法 >>

1. 鮑魚打開、由罐頭中取出後，先摘除鮑魚四週之雞冠形邊皮，再橫面切成適當之圓形薄片。
2. 小青江菜剝除外葉數枚後，留菜心，在半鍋開水中燙煮半分鐘，撈出、沖涼、瀝乾；玉米筍切斜段、也川燙一下。
3. 洋菇去蒂、切成橫片；蘆筍切兩段備用。
4. 將炒鍋燒熱，放下2大匙油，先倒下洋菇片拌炒，並注入清湯和罐中之鮑魚湯1/2杯，再加鹽、醬油調味，煮滾後，放下鵪鶉蛋、玉米筍及菜心，再煮滾後便可勾芡。
5. 落下蘆筍段一滾，即將全部材料盛到大盤內，而鍋中仍留下湯汁約1杯量，將鮑魚片倒下、再煮一滾便可起鍋，盛在盤中其他材料上。

金鈎魷魚絲
Shredded Squid with Pork

材料 >>
乾魷魚1條（約120公克）、鹼（2.5公分四方）1塊（或小蘇打粉2茶匙）、開水2杯、韭黃80公克、筍1支、紅辣椒2支、香菇3朵、瘦豬肉100公克、油5大匙

調味料 >>
酒1/2大匙、醬油（淡色）2大匙、鹽1/3茶匙、醋1/2大匙、麻油1/2茶匙

Ingredients
1 piece dried squid (about 120g.),
1 piece lye (2cm square) or 2 tsp. baking soda,
2 cups boiling water,
80g. yellow leeks,
1 bamboo shoot (cooked),
2 red chilies,
3 black mushrooms,
100g. lean pork,
5 tbsp. oil

Seasonings
1/2 tbsp. wine,
2 tbsp. light colored soy sauce,
1/3 tsp. salt,
1/2 tbsp. vinegar,
1/2 tsp. sesame oil

Procedures
1. From the sharp point, roll the squid into a roll, then cut the squid into thin strips. Put it in a big bowl with the lye or baking soda. Add boiling water and mix well. Soak for 30 minutes. Then rinse it for several times.
2. Cut the leeks into 3cm sections. Cut the bamboo shoot into thin strips. Then cut the red chilies and pork into the same size strips.
3. Heat 2 tbsp. oil in a pan. Stir fry the soaked squid for about 5 seconds. Then remove. The squid should be all curled.
4. Heat 2 tbsp. oil in a pan. Stir fry the pork. Add the black mushroom, bamboo shoot and red chilies, stir evenly. Then add the squid, wine, soy sauce, and vinegar, stir fry for a few seconds. Finally, add the leeks. Turn off the heat, mix again, splash sesame oil and remove to a plate to serve.

做法 >>

1. 將魷魚由尖頭緊緊捲起，切成細絲，切好全部放在大碗內，加入鹼塊或小蘇打粉，沖下開水拌合，大約浸泡30分鐘，再以清水洗淨待用（中途應再添加熱水1/2杯）。
2. 韭黃切成3公分長之段；筍煮熟後切絲；紅辣椒、豬肉和香菇均分別切絲備用。
3. 油2大匙燒熱後，將魷魚絲傾入鍋中，用旺火急炒約5秒鐘，見魷魚絲捲曲即盛出。
4. 另用油2大匙炒肉絲、香菇絲、紅辣椒絲和筍絲等，炒勻後，再將魷魚絲倒下，並淋下酒、醬油、鹽及醋炒合。倒下韭黃，關火後，略加鏟拌數下，滴下麻油少許即可。

熗墨魚花
Cuttlefish Salad

材料 >>
新鮮魷魚（或墨魚）2條、小白菜（或小黃瓜）150公克、水發木耳1/2杯、蔥屑2大匙、嫩薑屑1大匙

調味料 >>
醬油2大匙、醋2大匙、麻油2大匙、鹽1/3茶匙、胡椒粉少許

芥末汁 >>
芥末粉1大匙、酒1/2大匙、溫水1大匙

做法 >>
1. 將魷魚剝去薄皮後，在內面部份切上交叉之細斜刀紋，再分切成2.5公分四方菱角小塊備用。
2. 小白菜切成2.5公分長小段；木耳摘洗乾淨備用。
3. 芥末粉加酒及溫水調成稠汁後，蓋嚴、燜3分鐘，使其透出辣味。
4. 將所有調味料及蔥、薑屑均放入芥末汁小碗內，調勻成調味汁。
5. 燒一鍋開水後，先放下小白菜燙熟（約20秒鐘），隨後加入木耳，再10秒鐘後全部撈出，放在大碗內，用一半量之調味汁拌勻，盛在碟中。
6. 再把鍋中之水重加燒開，投下切好之魷魚塊，以大火燙熟（約10秒鐘），撈出後也用調味汁拌勻，迅速盛放在小白菜上即可上桌。

 這是一道熱拌菜，也可以用蝦仁或蛤蜊來代替。

This is a hot salad dish. Instead of squid, clams or shrimps may be used.

Ingredients
2 fresh squid (or cuttlefish), 150g. green vegetable, 1/2 cup soaked fungus, 2 tbsp. chopped green onion, 1 tbsp. chopped young ginger

Mustard paste
1 tbsp. mustard powder, 1/2 tbsp. wine, 1 tbsp. warm water

Seasonings
2 tbsp. light colored soy sauce, 2 tbsp. brown vinegar, 2 tbsp. sesame oil, 1/3 tbsp. salt, 1/4 tbsp. black pepper

Procedures
1. Remove the membranes from the squid. Score the inside lengthwise and crosswise; then cut it into diamond-shaped pieces of 2.5cm wide.
2. Cut the green vegetable into 2.5cm sections. Clean the fungus and tear it into small pieces.
3. Mix the mustard paste in a small bowl, cover and let stand for 3 minutes.
4. Add the chopped green, ginger, and seasonings to the mustard paste. Mix well.
5. Boil the green vegetable in the boiling water for 20 seconds, add the fungus, boil for another 10 seconds. Remove and drain. Mix with 1/2 of the mustard seasoning sauce. Place on a plate.
6. Bring the same water to a boil again. Add the squid. Boil over high heat for about 10 seconds. Remove and mix with the remaining mustard seasoning sauce. Pour it over the vegetable. Serve.

鴛鴦蝦仁

Stir-fried Lovers Shrimp

材料 >>

新鮮蝦仁450公克、豆苗（或嫩西洋菜）150公克、蔥小段20支、薑小片20片、蕃茄醬3大匙、油1杯

醃蝦料 >>

蛋白1大匙、太白粉1大匙、鹽1/4茶匙

調味料 >>

酒1大匙、鹽1/3茶匙、麻油1/4茶匙

做法 >>

1. 蝦仁先用鹽捏洗，再用多量水沖淨，瀝乾水份後再用紙巾盡量吸乾水分。用調好的醃蝦料拌勻，醃半小時以上（久一點較好）。
2. 將豆苗或西洋菜炒熟後（加鹽少許調味），盛出放在餐盤的中間（如用西洋菜應先在開水內燙過再炒）。
3. 炒鍋燒熱，放下1杯油，待油熱至8分熱時，將蝦仁全部倒下，用大火泡熟（約20秒鐘），見蝦仁變白即撈出，將油全部倒出。
4. 另放回1大匙油在炒鍋中燒熱，用大火先爆香蔥段與薑片，並將蝦仁重落鍋中，馬上淋下調勻的調味料，大火拌炒均勻，盛出一半放在餐盤中。
5. 將蕃茄醬淋下鍋中，與另一半之蝦仁同炒，鏟拌均勻便馬上盛出，放在盤中之另一邊，如此則紅、白分明，又鮮嫩可口。

Ingredients

450g. shelled shrimp, 150g. snow pea sprouts (or spinach or boiled broccoli), 20 pieces green onion (1/2" long), 20 slices ginger (1/2" square), 3 tbsp. ketchup, 1 cup oil

To marinate shrimp

1 tbsp. egg white, 1 tbsp. cornstarch, 1/4 tsp. salt

Seasonings

1 tbsp. wine, 1/3 tsp. salt, 1/4 tsp. sesame oil

Procedures

1. Clean the shrimp with a little of salt and then rinse with water. Drain and pat dry with paper towel. Marinate with mixed marinades for half an hour (the longer, the better).
2. Trim and stir fry the snow pea sprouts with a little of oil and salt for a few seconds. Remove and put in the center of a serving platter.
3. Heat 1 cup of oil in a frying pan (about 160ºC). Stir fry the shrimp for 15 seconds over high heat. When the shrimp turns white, remove and drain off the oil from the pan.
4. Heat 1 tbsp. oil to stir fry the green onion and ginger for a few seconds; add the shrimp and stir quickly. Pour in the mixed seasonings, mix thoroughly. Remove half of the shrimps to the serving platter.
5. Add the ketchup into the pan and stir fry with the other half of the shrimps for a few seconds. Remove immediately. Put on the other side of the platter. Serve hot. This is a very popular dish, it tartes tender and looks pretty.

豆 腐 蛋

有關豆腐、蛋類

　　豆腐及其加工品如：豆腐乾、豆腐衣、干絲、黃豆芽、豆漿等，其原料均係採用黃豆所製成，故所含之蛋白質與脂肪以及維生素B的成份頗多，對人體之營養價值極高。豆腐之烹調法有涼拌、紅燒、煎、炸、貼、燴、燉、川、扒、釀、蒸等多種。唯豆腐本身無味，必需配以鮮美副料或較重口味之佐料始能入味可口。

　　蛋類也係人體不可缺少之營養食品，唯在中國宴席中僅用其做配料或佐料。蛋之烹調法，家常方式為炒、煎、滷、煮、川、蒸、烘、釀等數種。

　　蛋類除可即席烹調而食之外，也可加工製成燻蛋、茶葉蛋、鹹蛋等保存較久時日。

About Tofu and eggs

　　Tofu also called bean curd and related bean products: dried tofu, tofu skin, dried tofu strings, bean sprouts, soy bean milk all originate from soybeans. Bean products are high in protein and fat. They are nutritious. Tofu can be served cold and raw, stir fried, fried, deep fried, stewed, braised, sautéed, boiled, steamed, stuffed, etc.. Tofu itself has no flavor, therefore, it is necessary to add fragrant ingredients or ingredients with stronger flavors so the cooked tofu can absorb some of these flavors.

　　eggs are high in nutrition. eggs usually accompany other major ingredients. Usually, eggs are stir fried, fried, boiled, cooked with soy sauce, steamed, baked, stuffed, etc..

　　In addition to the above mentioned methods of cooking eggs, there are smoked eggs, tea soaked eggs, and salty eggs. These can be kept for a long time.

蟹肉扒豆腐
Tofu with Crab Sauce

材料 >>
豆腐2塊或嫩豆腐1盒、蟹肉1/2杯、蟹黃2大匙、薑屑1/2大匙、蛋白1個、蔥屑1大匙

調味料 >>
酒1大匙、清湯2杯、鹽2/3茶匙、太白粉水1大匙

做法 >>
1. 豆腐先切除硬邊（嫩豆腐則不用去邊），再切成長方片（約0.6公分厚），全部用開水燙煮1分鐘，撈出後將水份瀝乾。
2. 在炒鍋內燒熱2大匙油，先爆香薑屑再放下蟹肉，炒數下後淋下酒，馬上注入清湯，然後將豆腐輕輕落鍋，加入鹽調味，以小火燒煮3分鐘左右。
3. 淋下太白粉水勾芡，要輕輕拌鏟、使湯汁變成稠糊狀。然後再淋下打散之蛋白，並將蟹黃（切碎）也放下拌合。關火後撒下蔥花，即可輕輕盛入盤中。

Ingredients
1 box tender tofu,
1/2 cup cooked crab meat,
2 tbsp. cooked crab roe (optional),
1/2 tbsp. chopped ginger,
2 tbsp. egg white,
1 tbsp. chopped green onion

Seasonings
1 tbsp. wine,
2 cup soup stock,
2/3 tsp. salt,
1 tbsp. cornstarch paste

Procedures
1. Remove the hard edge from the tofu (not for the tender tofu). Then cut into 0.6 cm thick pieces. Boil the tofu in boiling water for 1 minute. Remove. Drain off the water.
2. Heat 2 tbsp. oil in a pan to stir fry the ginger and the crab meat. Stir fry for a few seconds; sprinkle in wine and pour in the soup stock immediately. Add the tofu gently and season with salt. Cook over low heat for about 3 minutes.
3. Thicken the soup with cornstarch paste gently. Sprinkle in the beaten egg white and add the chopped crab roe; stir until blended. Turn off the heat, sprinkle the chopped green onion on top. Remove to a platter. Serve.

鍋貼豆腐
Sautéed Tofu Sandwiches

材料 >>
豆腐4方塊、絞豬肉 80公克、麵粉1/2杯、炸油3杯、薑絲半大匙、蔥絲2大匙

拌肉料 >>
鹽1/3茶匙、酒1茶匙、太白粉1茶匙

調味料 >>
清湯1/2杯、淡色醬油1大匙、鹽1/4茶匙、太白粉水1/2大匙

做法 >>

1. 將絞豬肉中加入2茶匙水，在砧板上再加以剁爛後，放進碗內，再放入拌肉料用力攪拌成為泥狀。
2. 選購較硬的豆腐，每塊先切成3公分寬、5公分長，再橫面片成4片（大約0.6公分厚）共計16片。
3. 在每片豆腐上撒下少許麵粉，再將肉泥1茶匙鋪在8片的豆腐上，而用另外一片豆腐蓋在肉泥上，做成夾心狀（可做8個），然後每個外面都沾滿麵粉。
4. 將油燒熱後，投下夾心豆腐、小火炸3分鐘撈出。
5. 另用1大匙油爆香薑絲，再加入清湯煮滾，用鹽及醬油調味後，放下豆腐用小火燜煮1分鐘，然後用太白粉水勾成薄芡，撒下蔥絲便可上桌。

Ingredients
4 pieces tofu,
100g. ground pork,
1/2 cup flour,
3 cups oil for deep fry,
1/2 tbsp. shredded ginger,
2 tbsp. shredded green onion

To mix with pork
1/3 tsp. salt,
1 tsp. wine,
1 tsp. cornstarch

Seasonings
1/2 cup soup stock,
1 tbsp. light colored soy sauce,
1/4 tsp. salt,
1/2 tbsp. cornstarch paste

Procedures

1. Chop the pork with 2 tsp. cold water. Place it in a bowl. Mix with salt, wine, and cornstarch.
2. Slice each tofu horizontally into four equal pieces about 3×5 cm rectangles and 0.6cm thick. All together are 16 pieces.
3. Sprinkle some flour on each piece of tofu. Spread 1 tsp. pork mixture evenly over 8 pieces of tofu. Then put another piece of tofu to cover the pork mixture. Make 8 stuffed tofu. Coat each stuffed tofu with flour.
4. Heat 3 cups of oil to deep fry the tofu sandwiches over low heat until light brown. Remove and drain.
5. Heat 1 tbsp. oil to stir fry the ginger for a few seconds. Add the soup stock, soy sauce, and salt, put in the fried tofu; stew over low heat for 1 minute. Thicken with cornstarch paste and sprinkle in the shredded green onion. Remove to a plate. Serve hot.

 夾好肉泥之豆腐也可沾上麵粉後，用平底鍋，在少量的油內煎黃兩面。
After dipping the tofu sandwiches in flour, you can fry them in a flat pan with less oil.

家常豆腐
Sautéed Tofu, Family Style

材料 >>

嫩豆腐（8公分四方）4塊、炸油3杯、絞豬肉60公克、大蒜屑2茶匙、薑屑1茶匙、蔥花1大匙

調味料 >>

辣豆瓣醬1大匙、清湯2/3杯、鹽1/3茶匙、糖1/2茶匙、麻油1/2茶匙、太白粉水1大匙

Ingredients

4 pieces tender tofu (8 × 8 cm) ,
3 cups oil for deep fry,
60g. ground pork or beef,
2 tsp. chopped garlic,
1 tsp. chopped ginger,
1 tbsp. chopped green onion

Seasonings

1 tbsp. hot bean paste,
2/3 cup soup stock,
1/3 tsp. salt,
1/2 tsp. sugar,
1/2 tsp. sesame oil,
1 tbsp. cornstarch paste

Procedures

1. Cut the tofu into 4cm square pieces. Cut each square piece into two triangles. Then cut each piece horizontally so that each piece is about 1.5cm thick.
2. Heat the oil in a pan; deep fry the tofu until it is golden brown. Remove the tofu and drain off the oil.
3. Heat 2 tbsp. oil in s pan; stir fry the pork; then add the hot bean paste, garlic, and ginger, stir fry until fragrant. Add the soup stock and season with salt and sugar, finally, add the tofu. Cover the lid and cook over low heat for 3 minutes.
4. Thicken the sauce with cornstarch paste, add sesame oil and green onions on top at last. Remove to a platter and serve.

做法 >>
1. 豆腐先切除硬邊，再切成約4公分四方塊，然後對角切成三角形，並由中間橫面片開成為2片（約1.5公分厚）。
2. 將豆腐用燒熱之炸油炸上半分鐘，使外皮稍硬而呈金黃色為止，撈出後將油瀝乾。
3. 鍋中放2大匙油，先爆炒豬絞肉，至肉炒散後，再放下蒜屑、薑屑及辣豆瓣醬，繼續炒數秒鐘，注入清湯並放鹽、糖調味，再將豆腐落鍋，輕輕同拌，用小火燜煮3分鐘左右。
4. 將太白粉水慢慢淋入鍋中，並輕輕拌鏟均勻，淋下麻油數滴，並撒下蔥花，即可裝盤。

材料 >>
干貝2個、香菇5朵、全瘦火腿（切絲）半杯、老豆腐（8公分四方）6塊、清湯5杯、小青江菜6棵

調味料 >>
鹽2茶匙、太白粉水2茶匙

做法 >>
1. 將豆腐每塊切成4小塊之後，放在鍋內，加入3杯清湯及1茶匙鹽，用小火煮約半小時。
2. 干貝泡軟、撕散成絲，約有1/4杯；香菇泡軟、切絲，約有1/3杯。
3. 取一隻蒸碗，在碗底將幹貝絲、火腿絲與香菇絲排列整齊，然後將煮過之豆腐密密的緊壓著放在上面，並注入半杯湯汁（即鍋中煮豆腐之湯），移進蒸鍋內蒸約1小時（也可以再久一些）。
4. 將蒸好之豆腐扣出在大餐盤中，把炒軟的小青江菜圍在盤內。
5. 在鍋內煮滾2杯清湯，並加鹽1/3茶匙調味，然後淋下太白粉水勾芡，使汁黏稠後澆到豆腐燉上即可。

三鮮豆腐墩

Scallops, Ham, and Mushrooms with Steamed Tofu

Ingredients
2 dried scallops, 5 black mushrooms, 1/2 cup ham (shredded), 6 squares firmed tofu (8 × 8 cm), 5 cups soup stock (chicken), 6 pieces green vegetables

Seasonings
2 tsp. salt, 2 tsp. cornstarch paste

Procedures
1. Cut each tofu into four pieces. Put in a pan. Add 3 cups of soup stock and 1 tsp. of salt. Cook over low heat for half an hour.
2. Soak the dried scallop to soft, tear it apart, about 1/4 cup; soak black mushroom to soft, shred it finely, about 1/3 cup.
3. In a medium size bowl, arrange the shredded scallop, ham, and black mushrooms in the bottom. Then put the cooked tofu on top of them. Add 1/2 cup of soup stock (used for cooking the tofu). Remove to a steamer. Steam for 1 hour over medium heat.
4. Turn the steamed tofu pudding upside down on a platter. Stir fry the green vegetables and season with some salt. Then arrange them around the tofu pudding.
5. Bring 2 cups of soup stock to a boil; season with salt and thicken with cornstarch paste. Pour it over the tofu pudding and serve.

◁註 鮑魚絲、蝦米、熟蟹肉、蛤蜊均可代替干貝,但不要用新鮮干貝。
Instead of the dried scallops, shredded abalone, dried shrimps, cooked crab meat or fresh clams can be used. Don't use fresh scallops.

魚香烘蛋
Egg Omelet, Sichuan Style

材料 >>
雞蛋8個、豬肉（絞肉）80公克、荸薺5個、木耳1/2杯、辣豆瓣醬1大匙、薑屑1/2大匙、蒜屑1茶匙、蔥屑2大匙、油1杯

調味料(A) >>
鹽1茶匙、濕太白粉水1大匙

調味料(B) >>
淡色醬油1/2大匙、清湯1/2杯、糖1茶匙、鹽1/2茶匙、太白粉1茶匙、鎮江醋1茶匙

做法 >>

1. 將雞蛋在大碗內打散後，加入鹽和濕太白粉水（用1茶匙太白粉加1大匙水）用力再打鬆，至十分發泡為止。
2. 在鍋內燒熱1杯油，將上項打鬆之蛋汁倒下，蓋上鍋蓋，用小火烘煎約3分鐘（應時常轉動鍋子、使蛋烘得均勻）。見蛋已半熟而泡起之後，便將鍋中之油慢慢倒出。然後翻轉一面，再把蛋的另一面用小火烘黃（約3分鐘），烘好後馬上放在乾淨的砧板上，用利刀切成約3公分寬之菱形塊，排列在餐盤中。
3. 荸薺切成碎絲；木耳亦切成碎屑備用。
4. 起油鍋（約2大匙油），先爆炒肉末至熟，再放下薑、蒜、辣豆瓣醬、木耳和荸薺屑等炒香，繼加入調勻的調味料(B)，煮滾後，撒下蔥屑，澆到蛋上便可供食。

163

豆腐、蛋
培梅食譜 II

Ingredients

8 eggs,
80g. ground pork,
5 water chestnuts,
1/2 cup soaked fungus,
1 tbsp. hot bean paste,
1/2 tbsp. chopped ginger,
1 tsp. chopped garlic,
2 tbsp. chopped green onion,
1 cup oil

Seasonings (A)

1 tsp. salt,
1 tbsp. cornstarch paste

Seasonings (B)

1/2 tbsp. light colored soy sauce,
1/2 cup soup stock,
1 tsp. sugar,
1/2 tsp. salt,
1 tsp. vinegar,
1 tsp. cornstarch paste

Procedures

1. Beat the eggs in a bowl. Add the salt and the cornstarch paste (1 tsp. cornstarch mix with 1 tbsp. water). Beat the eggs until they are stiff.
2. Heat 2 cups of oil in a pan. Pour the egg mixture into the pan. Cover and fry it over low heat for about 3 minutes (shake the pan frequently, so the egg mixture won't stick to the pan). When the omelet is half done, turn it over and fry this side for another 3 minutes. When the omelet is done, place it on a clean platter and cut it into pieces.
3. Cut the water chestnuts and fungus into small pieces.
4. Heat 2 tbsp. oil to stir fry the pork. Add ginger, garlic, hot bean paste, fungus, and water chestnuts, stir fry until fragrant. Then add the mixed seasonings (B). When it boils, add the green onions. Pour the sauce on top of the omelet and serve.

三色如意捲
Tri-color Egg Rolls

材料 >>
蝦仁250公克、肥豬肉80公克、香菇3朵、芥蘭菜葉4張、蛋2個

拌蝦料 >>
蔥1支、薑2片、酒1/2大匙、鹽1/3茶匙、胡椒粉少許、蛋白1大匙、太白粉1大匙

調味料 >>
鹽1/4茶匙、濕太白粉水1大匙

 此菜也可將芥蘭菜葉換成海苔而將香菇改為火腿條捲製。
Sea weed and ham shreds may be used in placed of the vegetable leaves and black mushrooms.

做法 >>

1. 將蝦仁抽去泥腸,用鹽抓洗、沖淨,拭乾水份,用刀面壓碎,再用刀鋒仔細斬剁,使成為蝦泥。肥肉也剁爛成泥狀,同蝦泥放一個大碗中。

2. 蔥和薑用刀拍碎,放在小碗內,加入酒1/2大匙及水1大匙,浸泡5分鐘備用。

3. 蝦泥中加入上項蔥薑汁及鹽、胡椒粉和蛋白,仔細順著同一方向攪拌至有黏性止,最後放下太白粉1大匙,續加拌勻備用。

4. 香菇泡軟去蒂、切成條狀;芥蘭菜葉在開水中燙過,撈出、沖涼、擠乾備用。

5. 將蛋2個打散,加入1/4茶匙鹽和1大匙濕太白粉水(用1茶匙太白粉加1大匙水),調勻後,在炒鍋內攤煎成一大張蛋皮,鏟出後整修成大方形。(約25公分長)

6. 在蛋皮上撒下少許太白粉,然後將半份蝦泥平均塗抹上去,再撒下少許太白粉,平鋪上一層菜葉,然後將所餘的蝦泥塗上,並將切成條狀之冬菇排在兩端、各成一直線,由兩端分別慢慢捲向中間,接面處用蝦泥少許黏住,移置菜盤中,上鍋以中火蒸熟(約10分鐘)。

7. 蒸熟之如意捲可以裹上麵粉糊炸脆、再切段裝盤或不用油炸、只切成寬片排盤也可。

Ingredients
250g. small shrimp (shelled),
80g. pork fat,
3 black mushrooms,
4 pieces green vegetable leaf,
2 eggs

To mix with shrimp
2 stalks green onion,
3 slices ginger,
1/2 tbsp. wine,
1/3 tsp. salt, a pinch of pepper,
1 tbsp. egg white,
1 tbsp. cornstarch

Seasonings
1/4 tsp. salt,
1 tsp. cornstarch paste

Procedures
1. Sprinkle some salt on shrimp and mix well. Rinse several times and then drain it dry. Smash shrimp to make paste. Chop the ground pork fat again and mix it with shrimp paste in a large bowl .
2. Pound the green onion and ginger and place it in a small bow, add 1 tbsp. water and 1/2 tbsp. wine, soak for 5 minutes.
3. Pour water from above mixture into the bowl of minced shrimp, then add the salt, pepper and egg white, stir well in one direction until sticky and smooth. Add 1 tbsp. cornstarch at last and stir again.
4. Soak the mushrooms to soft. Drain, remove the stems, and shred into thin slices. Boil the green vegetables for 3 seconds. Plunge it in cold water and squeeze dry.
5. Beat 2 eggs. Add salt and cornstarch paste (mix 1 tsp. cornstarch with 1 tbsp. water first). Make it into a thin pancake (about 25cm) Remove and cut it into a large square.
6. Sprinkle some cornstarch on the pancake. Spread 1/2 of shrimp mixture evenly over pancake and sprinkle some cornstarch on it. Spread the vegetable leaves and the rest of the shrimp mixture on it. Finally, put the mushroom shreds into 2 rows along the two ends. From these two ends, slowly roll pancake toward the center and seal together with some shrimp paste. Place upon oblong dish and steam for about 10 minutes.
7. Remove and cut into slices. Arrange on plate attractively. (you may make a flour-batter, dip the whole shrimp roll into the mixture and deep fry until golden brown, then cut it into slices).

中式蛋包
Chinese Rice Omelet

材料 >>
鹹肉丁3大匙（或用火腿、臘肉、香腸代替）、蝦米丁2大匙、榨菜丁1大匙、冬菇丁2大匙、蔥粒2大匙、米飯（或糯米飯）2杯、油4大匙

做蛋皮料 >>
蛋4個、太白粉1大匙、水3大匙

調味料 >>
酒1大匙、鹽1/2茶匙、糖1/3茶匙

 此菜可做為主食，也可切得大塊一些，做為自助餐或野餐最為適宜。
This dish is good for a buffet or a picnic.

做法 >>
1. 鍋中燒熱4大匙油，爆香蔥粒後，放下鹹肉丁炒至肉熟後加入冬菇、蝦米及榨菜等丁同炒，並淋酒、加調味料，再將米飯下鍋同炒，待所有材料和米均炒均勻時，即可盛出。
2. 將蛋打散，加入太白粉及水（先調勻），再調拌均勻。將砂鍋（或平底鍋）燒熱後，用刷子或布塗刷一層油，隨後倒下一半的蛋汁，馬上提起鍋子搖轉，把蛋汁平均攤開，成為20公分直徑大小之蛋餅。將所餘之蛋汁相同的做好另一個蛋餅。
3. 將做好的蛋餅置砧板上，放入適量的米飯在中間部分，成為細長一條，然後將四邊折合，使成為小枕頭狀之蛋包。
4. 鍋內燒油4大匙，將蛋包放入略煎一下，呈微黃色即成。
5. 每個蛋包切成3公分寬之段狀，分別排列在大盤內上桌（在盤之中間可放泡菜或好看之蔬菜點綴）。

Ingredients
3 tbsp. diced ham (or bacon or sausage),
2 tbsp. chopped dried shrimp,
1 tbsp. diced pickled mustard (or salted vegetables),
2 tbsp. diced black mushrooms,
2 tbsp. diced green onion,
3 cups cooked rice or glutinous rice,
4 tbsp. oil

For egg pancake
4 eggs,
1 tbsp. cornstarch,
3 tbsp. water

Seasonings
1 tbsp. wine,
1/2 tsp. salt,
1/3 tsp. sugar

Procedures
1. Heat 4 tbsp. oil in a pan and stir fry green onion for a few seconds; add ham, stir for about half a minute. Then add mushrooms, dried shrimp, pickled mustard, sprinkle wine, add seasonings. Pour in the prepared cooked rice and mix them well.
2. Beat 4 eggs with a mixture of cornstarch and water (mix together first), mix well. Heat a pan and brush lightly with oil. Pour 1/2 of egg mixture into the pan and lift the pan gently to allow the egg mixture to from a pancake about 20cm in diameter. Make 2 egg pancakes.
3. Place the egg pancake on a cutting board. Put 1/2 of rice mixture in the center and fold the two opposite edges of it into a roll.
4. Heat 4 tbsp. oil in a flat pan. Fry the egg roll. Turn over once. Fry until golden brown. Remove. Then cut into 3cm wide pieces.
5. Repeat this procedure to make the other omelet. Place on a plate and garnish with some pickled cabbage or lettuce along edge of the plate for color.

什錦蛋派
Assorted Meat in Egg Pie

材料 >>
雞肉（切丁）1/3杯、火腿1/4杯、鴨肫1個、小蝦仁1/4杯、香菇丁1/4杯、筍丁1/4杯、青豆2大匙、雞蛋8個、油8大匙

調味料(A) >>
酒1/2大匙、鹽1/3茶匙

調味料(B) >>
麵粉2大匙、鹽1/4茶匙、雞粉少許

Ingredients
1/3 cup diced chicken meat,
1/4 cup diced ham,
1 duck gizzard,
1/4 cup small shelled shrimp,
1/4 cup diced black mushrooms,
1/4 cup bamboo shoots,
2 tbsp. green peas,
8 eggs,
8 tbsp. oil

Seasonings (A)
1/2 tbsp. wine,
1/3 tsp. salt

Seasonings (B)
2 tbsp. flour,
1/4 tsp. salt,
1/6 tsp. chicken powder

Procedures

1. Cut the soaked black mushrooms, cooked ham, duck gizzard, chicken meat, shrimp and bamboo shoot into small cubes. Stir fry all the diced ingredients with 2 tbsp. oil and season with seasonings (A). Then add the green peas. Mix well. Remove and place in a bowl.
2. Beat the egg whites with an egg beater or chopsticks until very stiff. Add the seasonings (B), and egg yolks. Mix well.
3. Heat the pan to very hot. Add 6 tbsp. oil in the pan and then pour in the egg paste. Fry over low heat until almost stiff. Sprinkle the fried stuffing over the egg pie. Continue to fry until golden. Turn over and fry the other side for about 2~3 minutes.
4. Remove and cut the egg pie into triangles. Serve.

做法 >>
1. 將泡軟之香菇，及火腿與鴨肫、雞肉、蝦仁、筍（已煮熟）等各種材料全部分別切成小粒狀（如豆子大小），全部用2大匙油炒熟（並加鹽、酒各少許）再將青豆拌入，盛碗內備用。
2. 將雞蛋打開，把蛋黃與蛋白分別盛在兩個碗中，先用力將蛋白打至發泡（用打蛋器或多支竹筷）並加入麵粉、鹽和雞粉，再倒下蛋黃混合調勻備用。
3. 將鍋子燒熱後倒下油6大匙，隨即將蛋糊全部傾入，用小火煎炸，待固定了大小及形狀後，再將炒好之配料撒下，續煎片刻，見呈金黃色時翻一面再煎，大約2、3分鐘，至蛋派已熟即可。
4. 用餐盤將蛋派盛好（切成三角形小塊），即可上桌。

蝦仁蒸蛋

Shrimp with Steamed Egg

材料 >>
雞蛋4個、小蝦仁10隻、香菜1支

調味料 >>
冷清湯1 1/2杯、鹽1/2茶匙、酒1茶匙、雞粉少許、淡色醬油1茶匙

做法 >>
1. 將蛋在大碗內打散（不可打出泡沫來），慢慢加入調味料後調勻，用一個細紗網或篩子全部過濾一次。
2. 小蝦用鹽水漂洗一下、瀝乾。
3. 將第一項之蛋汁盛在一個蒸碗內（留下約1/4杯的蛋汁），放進蒸鍋中。先用大火蒸約2～3分鐘後改為小火慢蒸，約12～15分鐘左右見蛋汁表面已凝固。
4. 放下蝦仁和香菜，並倒下預留的蛋汁，繼續蒸至熟。食時整碗端上桌即可。

Ingredients
4 eggs, 10 shrimp (shelled),
1 stalk cilantro

Seasonings
1 1/2 cups soup stock (cold),
1/2 tsp. salt,
1 tsp. wine,
1/4 tsp. chicken powder (optional),
1 tsp. light colored soy sauce

Procedures
1. Lightly beat the eggs in a bowl. Add the seasonings; mix well. Pour the mixture through a sieve.
2. Clean the shrimp with a little salt and rinse with water. Then drain and pat dry.
3. Pour the egg mixture to a bow, reserve about 1/4 cup of egg mixture. Place the bowl into a steamer, steam over high heat for about 2~3 minutes. Then reduce the heat to low and continue to steam for about 12~15 minutes until the surface is firmed.
4. Place shrimp and parsley on top of steamed egg, then pour the reserve a egg mixture in, continue to steam until done. Remove and serve.

涼拌干絲
Dried Tofu Strips Salad

材料 >>
干絲300公克、芹菜 1-2支、胡蘿蔔絲1/4杯、小蘇打1茶匙

調味料 >>
鹽1茶匙、麻油2大匙、雞粉少許、辣油1大匙

做法 >>

1. 在鍋內燒開6杯水後，加入小蘇打或鹼粉一茶匙（如用鹼塊，一粒花生米大小即夠），隨即將干絲放下燙煮，約5～10秒鐘左右，見干絲已泛白而變得滑嫩時（可用指甲試切），即用漏勺全部撈出，沖過冷水洗淨，再用冷開水泡過，隨後完全瀝乾，盛在大碗內。
2. 芹菜去根葉後切成3公分長段，也在燙過干絲之開水中燙約10秒鐘，撈出後用冷開水沖涼、擠乾，也放入大碗中。
3. 胡蘿蔔絲用鹽少許拌醃10分鐘後擠乾，放入干絲中一起拌合均勻。
4. 加入調味料在干絲中仔細上下拌勻便可，食時裝盤上桌。

Ingredients
300g. thin dried tofu strips,
1~2 stalks celery,
1/4 cup carrot shreds,
1 tsp. baking soda

Seasonings
1 tsp. salt,
2 tbsp. sesame oil,
1/4 tsp. chicken powder (optional),
1 tbsp. red chili oil

Procedures

1. Boil 6 cups of water in a pot; add baking soda; then add tofu strips. Cook for about 5~10 seconds until the tofu strips turn very soft and light. Remove and rinse with cold water. Then drain and pat them thoroughly dry with paper towels. Place it into a large bowl.
2. Trim the celery, cut into 3cm sections. Boil for about 10 seconds in the baking soda water. Remove and plunge into cold water. Squeeze dry. Put together with the tofu strips.
3. Mix the shredded carrot with a little bit of salt for about 10 minutes. Squeeze dry and add to the large bowl.
4. Add seasonings to the bowl; mix well with tofu strips. Transfer to a plate. Then serve.

1. 如無現成干絲可用老豆腐，壓擠掉一些水份、切細絲代用。
2. 此係川味小菜，清香爽口，可做為家常涼拌菜食用。

1. If you can not get the thin dried tofu strips, you can use hard tofu instead. Put a cutting board and other heavy things on top of the tofu for about an hour. This will remove a lot of the liquid content from the tofu. Then it can be cut into strips.
2. This is usually a family dish, but it can be used as one of the appetizers.

蔬菜篇

有關蔬菜類

　　蔬菜之種類根據氣候與土質，各國所栽培之種類略有不同，有時同樣名稱，卻因品種有異，在烹調時所使用之方式及切割形狀與烹飪時間等就有所差別。
　　蔬菜大體可分為：
1. 根莖類：如蘿蔔、胡蘿蔔、馬鈴薯、洋蔥、荸薺、薑、筍等。
2. 葉菜類：如白菜、菠菜、包心菜、青江菜、芥蘭菜、芹菜、生菜等。
3. 瓜果類：如蕃茄、黃瓜、茄子、冬瓜、四季豆、南瓜、豌豆等。

　　蔬菜可炒、可煮、可涼拌，也有些可以煎、炸。炒蔬菜需視其種類而時間不定，唯硬性綠色蔬菜（如芥蘭菜、西洋芹菜、青江菜、四季豆等）應先用開水燙煮一下，撈出、沖冷水之後再用油炒，可保持翠綠、鮮美而永不變色。如為軟性綠色蔬菜（像菠菜、生菜、青椒、豌豆夾等）則不必燙開水而直接大火快炒便可。所有蔬菜類均應先洗後切，以減少營養成分之流失。

About Vegetables

　　Vegetables depend heavily on the climate and the nature of the soil in a particular area. Sometimes, vegetables have the same name, but in different places they are not quite the same. Vegetables must be cooked according to their texture and shape. Timing is very important. Vegetables can be divided into the following major groups:
1. Root vegetables: turnips, carrots, potatoes, onions, water chestnuts, ginger, bamboo shoots.
2. Leafy vegetables: Chinese cabbage, spinach, cabbage, broccoli, celery, lettuce, etc..
3. Fruit vegetables: tomatoes, cucumbers, egg plant, winter melon, string beans, pumpkins, peas, etc..

　　Vegetables can be stir fried, boiled, or served raw and cold. Other can be fried or deep fried. If the vegetables are hard (broccoli, western celery, green cabbage, string beans, etc.), they should be boiled in boiling water for about 30 seconds and then plunged into cold water. Then they can be stir fried. This method maintains the greenness and the fragrance of the vegetables. If one uses soft green vegetables (spinach, lettuce, green peppers, peas), just quickly stir fry them over high heat. Vegetables should be washed before they are cut to preseve their nutritional value.

釀蕃茄
Stuffed Tomatoes in Brown Sauce

材料 >>

蕃茄（紅而硬的）5個、豬絞肉200公克、蝦仁100公克、荸薺屑1大匙、油1/4杯、太白粉水2茶匙

拌肉料 >>

酒1大匙、鹽1/3茶匙、醬油1大匙、清水2大匙、胡椒粉少許

調味料 >>

糖2茶匙、醬油2大匙、清湯1/2杯

做法 >>

1. 蝦仁斬剁細爛之後與絞肉同盛大碗內，加入拌肉料及荸薺屑仔細拌勻。
2. 將蕃茄在開水內燙5秒鐘後，撈出；浸入冷水中、剝除外皮，直切為兩半，用小匙挖除籽與瓤，並在裡面撒下少許太白粉。將肉餡塞進去，並用手指沾水、抹平肉面。
3. 在鍋內燒熱油後，將蕃茄肉面向下、滑入鍋內，全部煎黃後取出，排列在蒸碗中（肉面向碗底），淋下調勻的調味料，移入蒸鍋中，用大火蒸約20分鐘。
4. 蒸好後端出，將汁先倒出在炒鍋內，然後把蕃茄扣覆在餐盤中。再將汁用太白粉水勾芡，澆到蕃茄上便成。

Ingredients

5 tomatoes (round and hard),
200g. ground pork (or beef),
100g. small shrimp (shelled),
1 tbsp. water chestnuts (chopped),
1/4 cup oil,
2 tsp. cornstarch paste

Seasonings (A)

1 tbsp. wine,
1/3 tsp. salt,
1 tbsp. soy sauce,
1/4 tsp. black pepper powder,
2 tbsp. water

Seasonings (B)

2 tsp. sugar,
2 tbsp. soy sauce,
1/2 cup soup stock or water

Procedures

1. Chop the shrimp and ground pork finely. Put into a bowl. Add chopped water chestnuts and seasonings (A), Mix well.
2. Blanch the tomatoes for about 5 seconds, remove the skin. Cut each tomato to halves. Scoop out the seeds and pulp with a spoon. Sprinkle a little of cornstarch on the inside of tomato. Then put the pork and shrimp into it. Smooth the surface of filling with a wet finger.
3. Heat 1/4 cup of oil in a frying pan, put the filled tomatoes in the pan (meat side down). Fry them until the meat side becomes brown. Remove and arrange in a bowl with meat side down. pour mixed seasonings (B) over the tomatoes. Place them into a steamer, steam for 20 minutes.
4. Pour the liquid out from the steamed tomatoes bowl into a small sauce pan, thicken it with the cornstarch paste. Turn the tomato balls from bowl to the serving plate and pour the sauce over it. Serve hot.

十錦涼菜
Chinese Salad, Rich Style

材料 >>

綠豆芽1 1/2杯、芹菜（切2.5公分長）1杯、胡蘿蔔絲1杯、白蘿蔔絲1杯、豆腐干絲1杯、木耳絲1/2杯、粉絲1杯、雞蛋皮絲1/2杯、熟豬肉絲1/2杯、熟雞絲1/2杯、春捲皮12張

綜合調味料 >>

醬油3大匙、醋1大匙、麻油2大匙、糖1茶匙、芥末醬1 1/2大匙

做法 >>

1. 胡蘿蔔及白蘿蔔切成3公分長的細絲後，分別用鹽1/2茶匙拌醃，約10分鐘後，沖過冷水加以擠乾。
2. 木耳及粉絲，分別用熱水泡軟後切成3公分長小段。
3. 芹菜與綠豆芽分別用開水各燙煮10秒鐘後撈出，隨即沖過冷水，並瀝乾（最好用手擠乾）。
4. 在一只小碗中調勻綜合調味料。
5. 將各種材料，分別而整齊的排列在大盤內，要各種顏色間隔排放，再與已蒸軟之春捲皮（或薄餅）及綜合調味料一起上桌。臨吃時，淋下調味料到大盤的菜上，仔細拌合均勻，用春捲皮捲裹而食便可。

Ingredients

1 1/2 cup bean sprouts,
1 cup celery (2.5cm long),
1 cup shredded carrot,
1 cup shredded turnip,
1 cup shredded bean curd dried,
1/2 cup shredded black fungus,
1 cup cellophane noodles,
1/2 cup shredded egg pancake,
1/2 cup shredded pork (cooked),
1/2 cup shredded chicken meat (cooked),
12 pieces egg roll wrapper

Seasoning sauce

3 tbsp. light colored soy sauce,
1 tbsp. vinegar,
2 tbsp. sesame oil,
1 tsp. sugar,
1 1/2 tbsp. mustard

Procedures

1. Cut the carrot and turnip into 3 cm long shreds. Mix them in separate bowls with 1/2 tsp. salt for about 10minutes. Rinse with cold water and then squeeze dry.
2. Soften the fungus and cellophane noodles in hot water. Then cut into 3 cm long shreds.
3. Boil the celery and bean sprout separately in boiling water for about 10 seconds. Remove and rinse with cold water. Then squeeze dry.
4. Prepare the seasoning sauce in a small bowl.
5. Arrange all of the ingredients in a pretty way on a large plate. Serve with seasoning sauce and warm egg roll wrappers. Pour the seasoning sauce over the ingredients and mix well just before eating. Take one egg roll wrapper, place some salad in the center, roll and fold one end, then eat.

雞絨蠶豆
Minced Chicken with Lima Beans

材料 >>
雞胸肉150公克、雞蛋白5個、蠶豆粒150公克、熟火腿屑1大匙

調味料 A >>
鹽1/3茶匙、酒1/2大匙

調味料 B >>
清湯2杯、鹽1/3茶匙、雞粉1/4茶匙、太白粉水1 1/2大匙

做法 >>
1. 雞肉除淨筋與皮，仔細剁爛成為泥狀，置入大碗內放下鹽及酒調拌，將雞蛋白一個放入碗中，同雞肉攪拌，至蛋白與雞肉混合之後，再放下第2個再攪拌，待5個蛋白全部攪勻為止。
2. 蠶豆粒傾入開水中燙煮20秒鐘（水中可加1/2茶匙小蘇打），撈出後、沖過水、瀝乾。
3. 起油鍋用2大匙油炒一下蠶豆後，注入清湯，並放鹽與雞粉調味，淋下太白粉水勾芡，至成糊狀時，將雞絨迅速傾入，並用炒鏟快加拌勻，馬上將火關熄。
4. 用一只深盤盛裝做好之雞絨蠶豆，再撒下火腿屑便成。

Ingredients
150g. chicken breast,
5 eggs (use egg white only),
150g. lima beans,
1 tbsp. chopped ham (cooked)

Seasonings (A)
1/3 tsp. salt,
1/2 tbsp. wine

Seasonings (B)
2 cups soup stock,
1/3 tsp. salt,
1/4 tsp. chicken powder,
1 1/2 tbsp. cornstarch paste

Procedures
1. Mince the chicken breast finely. Place in a bowl. Mix with seasonings (A) and 1 egg white. Mix well. Then add an additional egg white and mix well again. Repeat this procedure until all the five eggs white have been used up.
2. Cook the lima beans in boiling water for 20 seconds (you may add about 1/2 tsp. baking soda in water). Remove and rinse with cold water. Then drain and dry.
3. Heat 2 tbsp. oil in a frying pan. Stir fry the lima bean for a few seconds. Pour in the soup stock and season with salt and chicken powder, bring to a boil, thicken with cornstarch paste. Add the minced chicken meat. Stir quickly until thoroughly mixed. Turn off the heat immediately.
4. Pour onto a platter. Sprinkle chopped ham on top. Serve hot.

扒金銀菇

Braised Two Kinds of Mushrooms

材料 >>
小冬菇（或草菇）15個、洋菇1罐、青菜（豆苗或菠菜）250公克

蒸冬菇用料 >>
蔥1/2支、薑2片、醬油1大匙、糖1/2茶匙、油1大匙

炒洋菇用料 >>
清湯1杯、鹽1/3茶匙、糖1/2茶匙、太白粉水1大匙、牛奶水3大匙或鮮奶油2大匙

調味料 >>
酒1/2大匙、鹽1/4茶匙、太白粉水1/2大匙、鹽1/3茶匙

做法 >>

1. 選購同樣大小之冬菇（直徑約為3公分），全部用1杯溫水泡2小時至軟，切除蒂後置大碗中，加入蒸冬菇料及1杯泡冬菇的水（或高湯），上鍋蒸約20分鐘。

2. 洋菇從罐頭中取出，切除每一粒之菇蒂、使與菇底面相平後，用2大匙燒熱的油炒數下，然後注入清湯1杯，並放鹽，糖調味，煮滾一下，用調水之太白粉將汁芶芡成糊狀，再淋下牛奶水3大匙拌合，即裝入餐盤之半邊。

3. 另將油2大匙燒熱後，淋酒1/2大匙，即將已蒸過之冬菇連汁全部倒下（但要揀出蔥薑），再放鹽1/4茶匙，待煮沸後亦用太白粉水勾芡，盛入餐盤之另一半位置中。

4. 將洗淨之青菜用油炒過，並加適量鹽調味，盛出、排在盤之中間，以用做分隔兩種菇類即成。

Ingredients

15 small dried black mushrooms (or straw mushrooms),
1 can mushrooms,
250g. green vegetables

To steam black mushrooms

1/2 stalk green onion,
2 slices ginger,
1 tbsp. soy sauve,
1/2 tsp. sugar,
1 tbsp. oil

For mushrooms

1 cup soup stock,
1/3 tsp. salt,
1/2 tsp. sugar,
1 tbsp. cornstarch paste,
3 tbsp. milk or 2 tbsp. fresh cream

Seasonings

1/2 tbsp. wine,
1/4 tsp. salt,
1/2 tbsp. cornstarch paste,
1/3 tsp. salt

Procedures

1. Soak black mushrooms in 2 cups of warm water for about 2 hours and remove the stems (reserve the water). Place into a bowl and add green onion, ginger, soy sauce, sugar, oil and 1 cup of reserved mushroom water (or soup stock). Steam for 20 minutes.
2. Remove the mushrooms from can. Heat 2 tbsp. oil to stir fry the mushrooms. Add 1 cup of soup stock, season with salt and sugar, cook for about 1 minute. Thicken with cornstarch paste. Add milk and mix thoroughly. Pour on one side of the platter.
3. Heat another 2 tbsp. oil in a pan, sprinkle in 1/2 tbsp. wine and add steamed black mushrooms with the stock (remove the green onion and ginger). Bring to a boil and season with salt. Add cornstarch paste to thicken the stock. Remove to the other side of the platter.
4. Trim the green vegetables. Stir fry with oil, and season with salt. Place on the platter between the two different kinds of mushrooms.

 1. 亦可用新鮮洋菇，煮的時間約為3分鐘。
　　1. You may use fresh mushroom to make this dish, cook for 3 minutes for the fresh ones.

和菜戴帽
Stir-fried Vegetables Covered with Eggs

材料 >>
瘦豬肉200公克、韭黃100公克、菠菜（或青江菜）120公克、綠豆芽200公克、粉絲50公克、雞蛋3個、蔥段1支、大蔥段12小支、單餅（或春捲皮）12張

甜麵醬料 >>
甜麵醬2大匙、麻油1大匙、糖1大匙、水1大匙

醃肉料 >>
醬油1大匙、太白粉1大匙、水1大匙

調味料 >>
醬油2大匙、鹽1茶匙

 單餅的做法在培梅食譜第1冊第318頁。

Recipe for dan-bing is in Pei Mei's Chinese Cook Book Vol. I page 318.

做法 >>
1. 豬肉切成細絲，用醃肉料仔細拌勻，醃約15分鐘。
2. 粉絲用溫水泡軟後切短（約5公分長），將油2大匙燒熱後，放下蔥段爆香，加醬油2大匙及鹽1/4茶匙調味，放下粉絲和約1/3杯水燜煮片刻，再將綠豆芽加入，用大火急炒至豆芽脫生便好，盛出。
3. 將切成3公分長之菠菜用油2大匙略炒，加鹽1/3茶匙調味後盛入盤內。
4. 另起油鍋熱約3大匙油，將豬肉絲炒熟，並加入切成3公分長之韭黃，拌炒數下，加鹽少許調味，即熄火，將已炒好的菜倒下鍋中，與肉絲、韭黃混合拌勻，全部盛在一只大盤中。
5. 蛋打散後加鹽1/3茶匙，水1大匙及太白粉一茶匙（先調勻），在鍋內攤煎成一大張蛋皮，整張覆蓋在上項合菜上即可上桌。
6. 用兩只小碟分別裝蔥段（約5公分長）及甜麵醬料（甜麵醬等先以小火煮半分鐘，冷後裝小碟內），食時先用蔥段蘸甜麵醬塗抹在餅上，再將菜夾放在餅中捲裹而食。

Ingredients

200g. lean pork,
100g. white leeks,
120g. spinach (or green cabbage),
200g. bean sprouts,
50g. dried bean threads,
3 eggs,
1 stalk green onion,
12 sections scallion,
12 pieces dan-bing (or egg roll wrapper)

Sweet bean paste sauce

2 tbsp. sweet bean paste,
1 tbsp. sesame oil,
1 tbsp. sugar, 1 tbsp. water

To marinate pork

1 tbsp. soy sauce,
1 tbsp. cornstarch,
1 tbsp. cold water

Seasonings

2 tbsp. soy sauce,
1 tsp. salt

Procedures

1 Cut the pork into thin, long strings. Place in a bowl and marinate for about 15 minutes.

2 Soak the dried bean threads in warm water until soft. Cut into 5 cm long. Heat 2 tbsp.oil To stir fry green onion sections. Add soy sauce, 1/4 tsp. salt, bean threads and 1/3 cup of water, cook for about 1 minute. Add bean sprouts. Stir quickly over high heat until the bean sprouts are done (about 10 seconds). Remove to a platter.

3 Cut the spinach into 3 cm long. Stir fry with 2 tbsp. heated oil for a few seconds. Remove to the platter.

4 Heat another 3 tbsp. oil in the same frying pan; stir fry the pork strings to done. Add the white leeks and stir fry over high heat; season with 1/4 tsp. salt. Return all vegetables to pan, mix well then remove to a serving plate.

5 Lightly beat eggs with 1/3 tsp. salt, 1 tsp. cornstarch and 1 tbsp. water (mix cornstarch and water first). Make one thin pancake (about 20 cm round) in a frying pan. Put the egg pancake on top of stir fried dish.

6 Serve with scallion sections (or green onion sections) and sweet bean paste sauce on two small plate, and warmed dan-bing (or egg roll wrapper) to wrap the dish. This is do-it-yourself meal: Put one piece of dan-bing on an individual plate. Then pick up one piece of scallion with chopsticks and dip a little bit of bean paste sauce. Rub the bean paste on the dan-bing. Place 2 tbsp. the stir fried dish on it and fold one side toward center and eat.

蟹肉焗菜膽
Baked Chinese Cabbage with Crab Sauce

材料 >>
蟹肉1/2杯、蟹黃2大匙、大白菜800公克、麵粉4大匙、清湯2 1/2杯

調味料(A) >>
鹽1茶匙、糖1茶匙、雞粉少許

調味料(B) >>
鹽2/3茶匙、奶水3大匙或鮮奶油2大匙

Ingredients
1/2 cup cooked crab meat,
2 tbsp. cooked crab roe,
800g. Chinese cabbage,
4 tbsp. flour,
2 1/2 cups soup stock

Seasonings (A)
1 tsp. salt,
1 tsp. sugar,
1/4 tsp. chicken powder

Seasonings (B)
2/3 tsp. salt,
3 tbsp. milk or 2 tbsp. cream

Procedures
1. Remove the cabbage leaves. Rinse and cut into 5cm crosswise slices. Then slice into 1.5cm wide strips (leafy cabbage may be cut a little wider).
2. Heat 2 tbsp. oil in a frying pan; put the stem portions of the cabbage in the pan; stir fry for about 1 minute until almost softened. Then add the leafy cabbage. Stir fry again over high heat until soft. Season with seasonings (A). Cook until very tender. Remove the cabbage.
3. Heat 4 tbsp. oil to stir fry the flour for a few seconds. Pour in 2 1/2 cups of soup stock slowly. Stir until thickened. Add 2/3 tsp. salt, crab meat and crab roe. Mix well. Turn off the heat. Add the milk. Mix thoroughly. Remove half of the crab sauce to a bowl and reserve it.
4. Mix the cabbage with the remaining crab sauce; remove to a baking ware. Heat the oven to 240ºC, bake the cabbage for about 15 minutes until the surface becomes golden brown. Serve hot.

做法 >>

1. 將大白菜菜葉一瓣一瓣剝下後洗淨，先切成5公分長之段，再順紋切1.5公分的寬條（葉子可切得寬些）。
2. 在炒菜鍋內燒熱3大匙油後，先放菜莖部份略炒片刻，再放葉子下鍋，以大火炒至全部收軟，加入調味料(A)調味，然後繼續加以煮至喜愛的爛度，撈出白菜、瀝乾菜汁。
3. 將鍋洗淨，用4大匙油小火炒香麵粉，再慢慢淋下清湯拌成糊狀，加鹽2/3茶匙後落下蟹肉及蟹黃拌勻，熄火，加入奶水調合，先盛出一半在小碗內。
4. 將白菜傾入鍋中同奶油糊拌勻，盛入大碗或烤盆中，然後將預先盛出之另一半奶油糊澆在面上，移入預熱好的烤箱中，用240℃隔水烤約15分鐘，至表面上呈金黃色時便成。

羅漢齋

Assorted Vegetarian Dish

材料 >>
筍1支、小黃瓜1條、馬鈴薯1個、胡蘿蔔1/2支、洋菇10個、白花椰菜120公克、冬菇6個、素腸1條、油麵筋10個、冬瓜（或白蘿蔔）300公克、小玉米6支、白果1杯、紅棗8粒、鵪鶉蛋（煮熟的）10個、大通心粉1杯、清湯1杯

調味料 >>
醬油2大匙、鹽1/2茶匙、糖1茶匙、麻油1茶匙

Ingredients
1 bamboo shoot,
1 cucumber,
1 potato,
1/2 carrot,
10 mushrooms,
250g. cauliflower,
6 black mushrooms,
300g. winter melon or turnip,
8 pieces baby corn,
1 cup ginkgo,
8 red dates,
10 quail eggs (cooked),
1/2 cup macaroni,
1 cup soup stock (chicken)

Seasonings
2 tbsp. soy sauce,
1/2 tsp. salt,
1 tsp. sugar,
1/2 tbsp. sesame oil

Procedures

1 Cut the bamboo shoot, cucumber, potato, winter melon, carrot, cauliflower into small varied shapes, (all about the same size). Then put them into the boiling water following a sequence according to the degree of their hardness. Those hardest should be cooked first. Cook over high heat, until all become tender. Remove, and put them into cold water immediately. (the reason for doing so is to keep the original color of the vegetable)

2 Soak black mushrooms and red dates to soft; discard stems of black mushroom, and cut into appropriate size. Rinse ginkgo and drain.

3 Cook the macaroni in boiling water for about 6 minutes until tender. Remove and rinse with cold water.

4 Heat 3 tbsp. oil in a frying pan. Stir fry black mushrooms and mushrooms first for a few seconds. Then add all the other ingredients and the soy sauce, salt, sugar, and soup stock. Cook over high heat until the soup stock is absorbed. Add sesame oil and serve.

做法 >>

1. 將筍、小黃瓜、馬鈴薯、白花椰菜、胡蘿蔔、素腸、冬瓜等,分別切成不同形式之片狀或球狀,按硬度先後下鍋,用開水以大火燙煮至熟,並在撈出之後馬上用冷水沖泡,瀝乾備炒。
2. 冬菇、油麵筋、紅棗等均用溫水泡軟,備用。
3. 通心粉煮約5分鐘至無硬心為止,撈出後沖過冷水留用。
4. 起油鍋,用3大匙油先爆炒冬菇、洋菇等,隨後將各種材料全部放下,加醬油、鹽和糖調味,注入清湯,以大火燒煮至汁收乾時,淋下麻油即成。

三層塔
Quail Eggs and Mushrooms with Vegetables

材料 >>
小香菇15朵、小青江菜12支、鵪鶉蛋12粒、麵粉1大匙

蒸香菇用料 >>
醬油1 1/2大匙、蔥1支、薑2片、八角1顆、清湯1杯

調味料 >>
清湯1杯、鹽1/2茶匙、醬油2大匙

做法 >>

1 小香菇用溫水泡軟之後剪除菇蒂，放在碗中，加蒸香菇料後入鍋蒸20分鐘。

2 青江菜先用開水燙半分鐘、撈出泡過冷水再瀝乾水分。

3 加熱1大匙油炒青江菜，加入1杯清湯，大火煮約1分鐘，放下鹽調味後即撈起並瀝乾湯汁，排列在餐盤底成一圈。

4 將蒸過之香菇一個一個排列在青江菜上之內圈。

5 熟鵪鶉蛋擦乾水份放在盤中，淋下醬油2大匙、搖動盤子使蛋滾動而能全部沾上醬油，瀝乾醬油後撒上麵粉，然後用熱油炸成金黃色撈出。

6 將炸過之蛋也放進煮過青江菜之湯汁中一滾，全部堆放在香菇上成塔形。鍋中之汁則用太白粉水勾芡，淋在盤中三層塔上即可。

Ingredients

15 pieces dried black mushrooms (small sized),
12 pieces green vegetables,
12 quail eggs,
1 tbsp flour

To steam mushrooms

1 1/2 tbsp. soy sauce,
1 stalk green onion,
2 slices ginger,
1 star anise,
1 cup soup stock

Seasonings

1 cup soup stock,
1/2 tsp. salt,
2 tbsp. soy sauce

Procedures

1 Soak the black mushrooms in warm water until soft. Remove the stems. Place in a bowl. Add the condiments to steam for about 20 minutes.

2 Blanch the green vegetables in boiling water for about 30 seconds. Remove and plunge into cold water immediately. Drain and squeeze dry.

3 Fry the green vegetables with 2 tbsp. oil in a pan. Add 1 cup of soup stock. Cook over high heat for 1 minute and season with salt. Remove and drain off the soup; arrange on a platter.

4 Arrange the black mushrooms on the green vegetables, but don't cover the green vegetables.

5 Mix the soy sauce with the shelled eggs. Roll the plate, so the egg will cover by the soy sauce. Drain and cover the egg with flour. Deep fry them over high heat until golden brown. Drain.

6 Cook the fried eggs with the same sauce (No. 3) for a few second. Remove and put the eggs on the center of the black mushrooms. Thicken the sauce with cornstarch paste and pour over the eggs. Serve.

火腿冬瓜夾
Stuffed Winter Melon with Ham

材料 >>
冬瓜800公克、豬絞肉240公克、全瘦火腿100公克

拌肉料 >>
蔥薑水2大匙、鹽1/3茶匙、酒1茶匙、太白粉2茶匙、麻油1/2茶匙、胡椒粉少許

調味料 >>
清湯1杯、鹽1/3茶匙、白胡椒粉少許、太白粉水2茶匙

做法 >>
1. 將冬瓜削皮、除籽、去瓤之後，切成2.5公分寬、4公分長，一刀不斷、一刀切斷的活頁型，共12片備用。
2. 絞肉中加入拌肉料等佐料後，順著同一方向仔細攪拌至有黏性為止。
3. 火腿切成1.5公分寬、4公分長之薄片，共12片留用。
4. 在每一塊冬瓜的切縫中塞填肉餡約半大匙，並插放一片火腿片，全部做好後整齊的排列在一只中型蒸碗中，注入清湯1/2杯，移進蒸鍋中，以大火蒸20分鐘。
5. 將蒸好之冬瓜夾的湯汁泌出，冬瓜扣出在大餐盤內。
6. 湯之中再加入清湯1杯，並以鹽和胡椒調味，一起煮滾後再用太白粉水勾芡，將此汁澆到冬瓜夾上即成。

Ingredients
800g. winter melon,
240g. ground pork,
100g. Chinese ham

Seasonings (A) for pork
2 tbsp. green onion and ginger juice,
1/3 tsp. salt,
1 tsp. wine,
2 tsp. cornstarch,
1/2 tsp. of sesame oil,
1/4 tsp. black pepper

Seasonings (B)
2/3 cup soup stock,
1/3 tsp. salt,
1/4 tsp. white pepper,
2 tsp. cornstarch paste

蔬菜篇
培梅食譜 II

Procedures

1. Peel off the green rind and scoop out the seeds from the winter melon. Cut it into 2.5cm wide, 4 cm long, 0.5cm thick, but do not cut through the first cut, make it like a hot dog bun.
2. Mix the ground pork with the seasonings (A); stir it in one direction until the pork mixture is very sticky.
3. Cut the ham into 1.5cm wide, and 4 cm long thin slices (12 pieces).
4. Put 1/2 tbsp. the pork mixture and one slice of ham into each double sliced of the winter melon. Arrange all the stuffed winter melon in a bowl; add 1/2 cup of soup stock into the bowl, steam for 20 minutes.
5. Turn the winter melon upside down onto a serving platter (Pour out the soup from bowl first).
6. Bring 1 cup of soup stock and the soup from bowl to a boil, season it with salt and black pepper. Add cornstarch paste to thicken the soup. Pour it over the winter melon. Serve hot.

麻辣豆魚

Bean Sprout Rolls with Chili Sauce

材料 >>
綠豆芽300公克、豆腐衣3張

調味料 >>
芝麻醬1大匙、醬油2大匙、糖1/2大匙、麻油1/2大匙、醋1茶匙、蔥屑1/2大匙、壓碎芝麻（炒過）2茶匙、花椒粉1/2茶匙、辣椒油1/2大匙

做法 >>

1. 燒一鍋開水（約10杯），將豆芽放下，並加入鹽1茶匙，用大火燙煮10秒鐘即全部撈出，用冷開水沖涼，再用手擠乾。
2. 豆腐衣修去兩邊尖角成為長方形，包入豆芽適量（排放時應盡量順絲放），由手邊盡量捲裹得很緊，捲好後，接口向下放在碟中。
3. 在平底鍋內將1杯炸油燒到7分熱，放下豆腐衣捲（接口向下）用小火煎炸，需多翻面，以使顏色均勻。
4. 在一個碗內放下芝麻醬與醬油，慢慢調拌至十分均勻時，再加入糖等其他調味料，在上桌前澆到已切成小段而排列在碟中之豆腐衣捲（即豆魚）上面便成。

Ingredients
300g. bean sprouts, 3 pieces dried tofu sheet

Seasonings
1 tbsp. sesame paste, 2 tbsp. soy sauce, 1/2 tbsp. sugar, 1/2 tbsp. sesame oil, 1 tsp. vinegar, 1/2 tbsp. chopped green onion, 2 tsp. fried sesame seeds (ground), 1/2 tsp. brown pepper corn powder, 1/2 tbsp. hot red chili oil

Procedures

1. Add 1 tsp. of salt in 10 cups of boiling water. Boil the bean sprouts over high heat for 10 seconds. Remove and plunge into cold water. Then squeeze it dry.
2. Trim off the two angles from two sides of the dried tofu skin, make it into a rectangle shape. Arrange 1/3 of bean sprouts neatly on the skin, from the edge toward you, roll into a tight roll. Place on a plate (edge side down). Repeat this procedure to make two more rolls.
3. Heat 1 cup of oil in a frying pan to about 140°C. Fry the sprout rolls (edge side down) over low heat. Turn over the sprout rolls when they are golden brown. All sides should be golden brown. Remove and cut it into 2.5cm pieces. Arrange on a plate.
4. Mix the sesame paste with 2 tbsp. soy sauce in a small bowl. After mixing well, add the rest of the seasonings. Mix thoroughly. Pour it over the bean sprout pieces before eating.

湯品篇

有關湯類

在中國宴席菜品中,通常應包括清湯菜一種及濃湯菜一種,清湯菜多係用蒸或燉、煲等方式所製成,材料多半採用雞、鴨、鴿或其局部(如雞翅膀、雞腳、雞腿等)加上鮮美乾貨(如香菇、干貝、火腿等),經長時間以文火烹調而成,其湯味鮮美又清香,夏季則酌加冬瓜、筍片之類清淡菜蔬。

濃湯通常稱謂"羹",多以海鮮類或乾貨類(如魚翅、燕窩、鮑魚、海參等)所調製。濃湯除用澱粉類(如玉米粉、太白粉、綠豆粉、葛粉、豆粉、馬蹄粉、藕粉)勾芡使汁黏稠之外,也可採用西式濃湯之做法,用油炒麵粉,再注入清湯攪勻成為糊狀者。

中國菜中所用之清湯(又名高湯或上湯),大都採用雞骨或豬骨以小火燉煮而成,唯骨頭必需剁小後,先用開水燙過、洗去血水,始可放入滾水鍋中,用小火燉煮(約2小時以上)。

About Soups

In a Chinese banguet it usually includes a clear soup and a thick soup. Clear soups are usually made by steaming, boiling, simmering, etc.. Usually a whole chicken, duck, or pigeon is used, but the parts can also be used. In addition, dried ingredients like dried black mushroms, scallops, and ham are often added. Clear soups must be cooked for a long time over low heat until it tastes fresh and delecious and has a mild fragrance. In the summer, winter melon, slices of bamboo shoot or other flat taste vegetables are added.

Thick soups are usually called "keng". Often seafood or dried ingredients (shark's fins, swallow's nest, abalone, sea cucumber etc..) are used. Cornstarch is usually used to prepare thick soups, but the Western method of frying flour can also be used. In a little oil, fry some flour. Then add some clear stock. Stir well to prevent lumps from forming.

Usually, we made soup stock with chicken or pork bones, simmer them over 2 hours to get clear soup stock.

原盅燉什錦
Steamed Assorted Meat soup in Casserole

材料 >>
海參2條、干貝5粒、竹笙6支、熟豬肚1/4個、蝦仁200公克、蹄筋200公克、大白菜（或冬瓜或白蘿蔔）600公克、清湯6杯

拌蝦料 >>
蛋白1大匙、鹽1/3茶匙、胡椒粉1/4茶匙、太白粉1茶匙、酒1茶匙

煮海參料 >>
蔥1支、薑2片、酒1茶匙、冷水3杯

調味料 >>
鹽1茶匙、酒1/2大匙

做法 >>
1. 先將蝦仁剁碎成泥，放在大碗內，加入拌蝦料仔細拌成泥狀，擠成蝦球，投入滾水中燙熟，撈出（或選購現成的蝦丸，可以直接使用）。
2. 海參放小鍋中，加煮海參料煮滾後改小火煮3～5分鐘，取出沖涼，打斜切成片。
3. 干貝泡水1小時後，略撕散開。
4. 竹笙泡水至漲開，洗乾淨，切成約5公分的段；蹄筋切短，兩種分別放入滾水中川燙5～10秒鐘，撈出、瀝乾。
5. 豬肚切成寬條；大白菜切成約2公分的寬段，在滾水中燙至微軟，撈出放在燉盅內。
6. 白菜上排放各種材料，注入清湯至淹過各料，並加鹽和酒調味，再蓋上蓋子（或用玻璃紙封住），移到蒸籠中蒸約1小時。取出即可上桌分食。

Procedures
1. Chop the shrimp to very fine, place in a large bowl; mix well with all seasonings (A). Make shrimp balls; boil in boiling water until done, drain. (or you may buy the already made shrimp balls).
2. Put sea cucumber and seasonings (B) in a pot, cook for 3~5 minutes after it boils. Remove and rinse cold; slice both to large slices.
3. Soak the dried scallops for about 1 hour, tear apart.
4. Soak the dried bamboo mushrooms to soft, rinse to clean, cut into 5 cm sections; cut each pork tendon to two pieces; boil separately for about 5~10 seconds, drain.
5. Cut the pork stomach into wide strips; cut Chinese cabbage to 2 cm wide strips, boil until it becomes a little soft, drain and arrange on a steam bowl.
6. Arrange all kinds of ingredients on top of cabbage, add soup stock (the soup stock should cover the ingredients). Season with seasonings (C); cover the lid and steam for one hour. Serve hot.

Ingredients

2 sea cucumbers,
5 dried scallops,
6 dried bamboo mushrooms,
1/4 pork stomach (cooked),
200g. shrimp,
200g. soaked pork tendon,
600g. Chinese cabbage (or winter melon or turnip),
6 cups soup stock

Seasonings (A)

1 tbsp. egg white,
1/3 tsp. salt,
1 tsp. cornstarch,
1/4 tsp. pepper,
1 tsp. wine

Seasonings (B)

1 stalk green onion,
2 slices ginger,
1 tsp. wine,
3 cups water

Seasonings (C)

1 tsp. salt,
1/2 tsp. wine

註 什錦的材料可以選擇現成有的或個人喜愛的,但是生的材料要燙煮過,才能保持燉出來的湯汁清澈、鮮美。

You may choose any ingredients you like or you already have it. The key point is to blanch or boil those row ingredients before steam it, so the soup can keep clear and taste good.

百花鵪蛋湯

Stuffed Quail Eggs and Shrimp Ball soup

材料 >>
鵪鶉蛋10個、小蝦200公克（或蝦仁100公克）、肥肉30公克、豆苗或其他青菜100公克、高湯6杯

拌蝦料 >>
鹽1/3茶匙、酒1茶匙、蛋白1大匙、太白粉1大匙

調味料 >>
鹽1茶匙

Ingredients
10 quail eggs,
200g. small shrimp (or 100g. peeled shrimp),
30g. pork fat,
100g. green cabbage,
6 cups soup stock (chicken)

To mix with shrimp
1 tsp. wine,
1/3 tsp. salt,
1 tsp. egg white,
1 tbsp. cornstarch

Seasonings
1 tsp. salt

Procedures

1. Peel off the shell of the shrimp and de-vine it. Rinse for several times; drain and pat it dry. Mince the shrimp and pork fat. Then mix together with salt, wine, egg white and cornstarch.
2. Put the quail eggs in a bowl. Cover the eggs with cold water. Place into steamer and steam for about 8 minutes. Then soak the eggs in cold water for a while. Remove the shells and cut the eggs in half lengthwise. (or you may buy the cooked quail eggs).
3. Sprinkle a little of cornstarch on the surface of the eggs. Then place some shrimp mixture on it. Shape the shrimp mixture to match the egg to form a ball. Make all eggs. Arrange the eggs on a plate, steam over high heat for 5 minutes.
4. Bring the soup stock to a boil. Add green cabbage and salt. Pour the soup into a large serving soup bowl, then put the egg balls into the bowl and serve.

做法 >>
1. 小蝦剝殼、抽去泥腸後,洗淨瀝乾,與肥肉分別剁爛,同置一碗內,加入拌蝦料仔細拌勻。
2. 鵪鶉蛋連殼置大碗中,加冷水上鍋蒸8分鐘,倒掉碗中之水後泡在冷水中,再逐個剝除外殼,每個直面對剖為兩半。若購買已煮好且剝殼的鵪鶉蛋:直接切半即可。
3. 在蛋的切面上撒下少許乾太白粉,再將蝦仁餡約1茶匙的量塗在面上,並用手指沾水抹平,使成為半圓形。全部做好,排在菜盤內,上鍋大火蒸5分鐘。
4. 將高湯在鍋內煮滾,加入嫩青菜並放鹽調味,然後倒在大碗中,將蒸熟之鵪蛋輕輕放入湯中即可上桌。

什錦鍋巴

Popped Rice with Sea Food Sauce

材料 >>
熟豬肉（全瘦）100公克、蝦仁100公克、魷魚半條、火腿片10小片、筍1/2支、香菇（或草菇、洋菇）6朵、豌豆夾20片、蔥1支、鍋巴（5公分 四方）8片

調味料(A) >>
太白粉1茶匙、鹽1/4茶匙

調味料(B) >>
酒1大匙、清湯2杯、鹽1/2茶匙、醬油2大匙、太白粉水2大匙

做法 >>

1. 將肉切薄片；蝦仁洗淨、拭乾水份，用調味料(A) 拌醃片刻；魷魚洗淨去外膜後切細密交叉之花紋，再切成菱形塊。
2. 筍煮熟後切片；香菇泡軟、去蒂、打斜成薄片；豌豆片摘好。
3. 鍋中燒開水，將魷魚、蝦仁、豌豆夾等川燙5秒鐘，撈起。
4. 在炒鍋內燒熱油3大匙，放入蔥支和香菇炒香，淋酒1大匙，隨即注入清湯2杯，加鹽和醬油調味，並加筍片、火腿片以及燙過之各種材料，待煮滾後用太白粉水勾芡，改用小火保溫。
5. 將炸油在另一只鍋內燒得極熱，然後投下鍋巴（剝開成小片），用大火炸膨脹，需用炒鏟翻拌至顏色變黃而酥脆時撈出，馬上裝在深盆或大碗內，同什錦料（盛另一只碗中），一起迅速送上桌，馬上將什錦料澆在鍋巴上，當時必呈油爆之聲即可迅速分食之。

Ingredients
100g. lean pork (cooked),
100g. small shrimp (shelled),
1/2 squid, 10 slices ham,
1 bamboo shoot (cooked),
6 black mushroomss,
20 pieces snow pea,
1 green onion,
8 pieces popped rice (guo-ba)

Seasonings A
1 tsp. cornstarch,
1/4 tsp. salt

Seasonings B
1 tbsp. wine,
2 cups soup stock,
1/2 tsp. salt,
2 tbsp. soy sauce,
2 tbsp. cornstarch paste

Procedures

1. Cut the pork into thin slices. Rinse the shrimp and pat dry, mix with seasonings (A). Clean and remove the membranes from the squid; then score the inside lengthwise and crosswise. Cut it into diamond shaped slices.
2. Slice the cooked bamboo shoot; soak the black mushrooms to soft, remove the stems, and cut into slices; trim the snow peas.
3. Boil the squid, shrimp and snow peas in boiling water for about 5 seconds. Remove.
4. Heat 3 tbsp. oil in a pan. Stir fry the green onion and black mushrooms; sprinkle in wine, then pour in soup stock. Season with salt and soy sauce. Put the ham, bamboo shoot and all of the No.3 ingredients into the soup. After boiling again, thicken with cornstarch paste (2 tbsp. cornstarch and 2 tbsp. water). Reduce the heat to low to keep it in warm.
5. Heat about 4~5 cups of oil in another pan to very hot. Deep fry the popped rice over high heat until puffed and golden brown. Remove to a platter or a big bowl. Bring the rice to table and pour the hot ingredients mixture (in a bowl) over it. At this moment, it should sizzles. Eat it immediately when it is hot.

油條蠣黃羹

Oyster and You-tiao Potage

材料 >>
牡蠣（即蚵肉）300公克、蔥2支、薑3片、油條1支、蔥屑2大匙、香菜屑2大匙

調味料 >>
酒2大匙、清湯6杯、鹽1 1/2茶匙、太白粉水4大匙、胡椒粉少許

做法 >>
1. 首將牡蠣揀棄殼屑，加鹽少許，輕輕抓洗乾淨並瀝乾水份。
2. 在鍋內煮滾半鍋開水，放下1支蔥、1片薑及1大匙酒，然後將蠣黃倒下，用大火川燙約5秒鐘，撈出並加以瀝乾。
3. 油條切小片，放入烤箱中烤酥，取出、盛放在碗底。
4. 另在炒鍋內燒熱2大匙油，放下蔥支及薑片煎香，隨後淋下酒，馬上倒下清湯，待湯沸滾時加鹽調味，並用調水之太白粉勾芡，使湯稠濃成稀糊狀。
5. 將已燙過之蠣黃倒入鍋內，燴煮一滾，即刻熄火，倒在油條碗中，然後撒下香菜屑、蔥屑，並灑胡椒粉少許，趁熱送席。

1. 油條之做法在本書中第237頁。
2. 如無油條，可用餛飩皮或春捲皮切成小片炸酥代替，也可用米粉或粉絲炸鬆取代之。
3. 最好用小的牡蠣，如沒有小牡蠣時，可以將大的牡蠣切小來用。
4. 也可以用蛤蜊或小蝦仁代替牡蠣。

Ingredients
300g. oysters (small and shelled),
2 stalks green onion,
3 slices ginger,
1 piece you-tiao,
2 tbsp. chopped green onion,
2 tbsp. chopped coriander

Seasonings
2 tbsp. wine,
6 cups soup stock,
1 1/2 tsp. salt,
4 tbsp. cornstarch paste,
1/4 tsp. black pepper

Procedures
1. Put some salt in the shelled oysters. Mix them with fingers. Rinse with water until clean. Drain.
2. Boil 6 cups of water with green onion, ginger, and 1 tbsp. wine; then add the oysters and boil for about 5 seconds. Remove and drain.
3. Slice the you-tiao into small pieces; bake until brown and crispy. Place on the bottom of a large serving bowl.
4. Heat 2 tbsp. oil in a pan. Fry green onion and ginger slices until brown. Splash 1 tbsp. wine in; add the soup stock immediately; bring to a boil. Discard the green onion and ginger; season with salt and thicken with cornstarch paste.
5. Add the oysters into the potage, bring to a boil again over high heat. Remove to the serving bowl. Sprinkle the chopped green onion, coriander, and black pepper over it. Serve hot.

1. Refer to the recipe of you-tiao, please see page 237.
2. Instead of you- tiao, you may use some deep fried cellophane noodles wonton wrpper, or rice crispy.
3. It is better to use small oysters, but if not available, big ones may be chopped into small pieces.
4. Instead of oysters, fresh clams or fresh small shrimp may be used.

清燉銀耳牛肉湯
Beef Soup with White Fungus

材料 >>
牛肉500公克、蕃茄2個、乾白木耳20公克、紅棗10粒、蔥1支、薑3片、八角1顆、香菜1支

調味料 >>
酒1大匙、鹽1 1/2茶匙、胡椒粉隨意

做法 >>

1. 牛肉洗淨，整塊放入鍋中，加滾水7杯和蔥、薑、八角、酒一起煮滾，改小火再煮約1小時，取出牛肉，待冷後切成塊。
2. 白木耳泡軟、剪去蒂頭，用滾水川燙1分鐘，撈出；蕃茄用滾水燙半分鐘，剝除外皮，切成塊；紅棗沖洗一下。
3. 將牛肉湯中的蔥等撈棄，再放下牛肉、白木耳、蕃茄和紅棗，一起再煮約半小時，至喜愛的爛度，加鹽和胡椒調味即可，裝碗後撒下香菜段。

Ingredients

500g. beef,
2 tomatoes,
20g. dried white fungus,
10 red dates,
1 stalk green onion,
3 slices ginger,
1 star anise,
1 stalk coriander

Seasonings

1 tbsp. wine,
1 1/2 tsp. salt,
pepper

Procedures

1. Rinse the beef, put in a soup pot, add 7 cups of boiling water, green onion, ginger, star anise and wine, bring to a boil, cook over low heat for about 1 hour. Remove the beef, cut into pieces after it cools.
2. Soak white fungus to soft, trim off the hard ends, boil for 1 minute, drain. Boil tomato for 1/2 minute, peel off the rind; cut into pieces. Rinse red dates.
3. Remove green onion and ginger from beef soup, add beef, fungus, tomato and red dates, cook for another half an hour to the tenderness you prefer. Season with salt and pepper, remove to a soup bowl, add coriander, serve hot.

海鮮砂鍋
Seafood Hot Pot

材料 >>
魚肉150公克、鮮蝦10隻、蟹腿肉100公克、蛤蜊300公克、洋菇8~10粒、蛋餃或其他喜愛的餃類10個、凍豆腐2塊、青菜400公克、蔥1支、蕃茄1/2個、清湯5~6杯、蔥花或香菜末適量

調味料 >>
鹽、胡椒粉適量

做法 >>
1. 魚肉打斜切片；蝦子剝殼、抽砂腸，從背部剖開一刀；蟹腿肉解凍後快速沖洗一下，瀝乾水分，和蝦仁分別拌上少許太白粉備用。
2. 蛤蜊泡在薄鹽水中吐砂；洋菇沖洗、瀝乾；凍豆腐切塊。
3. 墊底的青菜如選用較耐煮的大白菜或高麗菜，可以和蔥段、蕃茄塊一起先煮3分鐘。
4. 將凍豆腐、洋菇和蛋餃下鍋煮一滾，再排上各種海鮮類，加鹽和胡椒粉調味，蓋上鍋蓋煮滾即可。關火後可按個人喜好撒下蔥花或香菜，趁熱上桌分食。

Ingredients
150g. fish fillet, 10 shrimp, 100g. crab legs, 300g. clams, 8~10 mushrooms, egg dumplings or other kinds of dumplings, 2 pieces frozen tofu, 400g. vegetables, 1 stalk green onion, 1/2 tomato, 5~6 cups soup stock, chopped green onion or coriander

Seasonings
salt and pepper to taste

Procedures
1. Slice the fish fillet; shell and de-vein the shrimp, make a cut on it's back; defrost the crab legs. Mix a little of cornstarch with crab legs and shrimp.
2. Soak clams in light salty water to remove sand from clam; Rinse mushrooms quickly, drain; cut frozen tofu to pieces.
3. Cut vegetables to suitable size. If you use Chinese cabbage or cabbage, which can cook with green onion and tomato in soup stock for 3 minutes, for those vegetables which can not cook too long, should add it to the soup at last.
4. Add frozen tofu, mushrooms, egg dumplings to soup, bring to a boil. Arrange all sea food to the hot pot, season with salt and pepper; cover the lid, bring to a boil. Turn off the heat, add chopped green onion or coriander as you like. Serve hot.

清湯雙捲
Soup with Double Rolls

材料 >>
絞豬肉（前腿肉）400公克、高麗菜葉（或大白菜葉）10張、豆腐衣5張、香菇6朵、清湯6杯

拌肉料 >>
淡色醬油1大匙、酒1大匙、鹽1/2茶匙、太白粉2茶匙

調味料 >>
鹽2茶匙

做法 >>

1. 豬肉置大碗內，加入拌肉料仔細拌勻。
2. 香菇泡軟，片切成2片。取一只中型蒸碗，將香菇片一字排列在碗的中間。
3. 在開水內燙軟整棵高麗菜之後，將菜葉一張一張剝下（共需10張），切除每張菜葉中間之硬梗部份，使成為7公分寬、10公分長之大小後，分別包捲肉餡約1大匙多，成為5公分多長之筒狀。光面向下全部排列在蒸碗中之半邊內。
4. 豆腐衣每張切成2等分，成為相同大小之三角形（共10小張），分別包裹肉餡，像枕頭狀，也全部排入碗的另半邊。
5. 注入清湯半杯後，上鍋蒸20分鐘。上桌前將蒸好之材料倒扣在大湯碗內，再注入已沸滾、且加鹽調味過之清湯即成。

Ingredients

400g. ground pork,
10 pieces cabbage leaf,
5 pieces dried tofu sheet,
6 black mushrooms,
6 cups soup stock

To mix with pork

1 tbsp. light colored soy sauce,
1 tbsp. wine,
1/2 tsp. salt,
2 tsp. cornstarch

Seasonings

2 tsp. salt

Procedures

1. Place pork in a bowl. Mix well with the condiments.
2. Soak black mushrooms to soft, cut each piece into two pieces. In a medium sized bowl, arrange the black mushroom slices in a column.
3. Remove and discard the core of the cabbage. Place the cabbage in a deep pot of boiling water and gently remove the softened leaves. (about 10 leaves). Cut the leaves into 7cm wide, 10cm long pieces (don't use the hard part of the leaf). Place 1 tbsp. pork mixture in center of a leaf, fold and roll it into a roll about 5cm long. Put it on one side of mushroom with smooth side down.
4. Cut the tofu sheet into 2 equal triangular slices. Place 1 tbsp. pork mixture in center and roll it into the same shape as cabbage roll. Arrange on the other side of mushroom (also with smooth side down).
5. Add 1/2 cup of soup stock to the bowl. Steam it for 20 minutes. Remove the steamed dish and turn it over onto a large soup bowl. Bring the soup stock to a boil and season with salt. Pour it into the bowl and serve.

蕃茄玉米羹
Tomato and Sweet Corn Soup

材料 >>

玉米醬（罐頭）1/2罐、蕃茄丁1杯、洋菇片1/2杯、青豆1/3杯、清湯或水6杯、油1大匙

調味料 >>

酒1/2大匙、鹽1茶匙、太白粉水4大匙、蛋白1個

做法 >>

1. 在炒菜鍋內燒熱油後，淋下酒爆香，隨即將清湯傾入，再將玉米醬也倒下攪勻。
2. 待煮至沸滾後放鹽調味，並將洋菇片及蕃茄丁、青豆也落鍋再煮滾一次，將火馬上改小，然後慢慢淋下用水調溶之太白粉水，並不停的用勺子攪動，見黏度適當即可。
3. 蛋白在小碗內先打散，再將碗提高，慢慢淋入湯中，關熄火後輕輕攪動一下，使全部材料均勻即可盛入大碗內上桌。

Ingredients

1/2 can sweet corn,
1 cup diced tomatoes,
1/2 cup mushroom slices,
1/3 cup green peas,
6 cups soup stock or water,
2 tbsp. oil

Seasonings

1/2 tbsp. wine,
1 tsp. salt,
4 tbsp. cornstarch paste,
2 tbsp. egg white

Procedures

1. Heat 2 tbsp. oil in a frying pan. Sprinkle in wine and then pour in the soup stock immediately. Then add the sweet corn and mix well. Cook until the soup boils again.
2. Season with salt. Then add mushrooms, tomatoes and green peas. When it boils again, reduce the heat to low, and thicken the soup with cornstarch paste.
3. Beat the egg white and pour it into the soup carefully. Turn off the heat immediately. Pour into a soup bowl and serve.

菠菜豆腐羹

Spinach and Tofu Soup

材料 >>
菠菜150公克、嫩豆腐1/2盒、洋菇片（或筍片）1/2杯、瘦豬肉100公克或火腿小片2大匙、清湯6杯

調味料 >>
鹽 1 1/2 茶匙、太白粉水4大匙、胡椒粉適量

做法 >>

1. 將菠菜洗淨，整支投入開水中，用大火燙10秒鐘，撈出後沖過冷水，並加以擠乾，用刀切成極細碎之屑狀。
2. 豆腐切成如同指甲大小之厚片狀；豬肉先煮熟，待冷後也切成小薄片備用。
3. 將清湯在鍋內煮滾後，放下筍片、肉片及豆腐，待再滾時，用調過水之太白粉慢慢勾芡，使湯成為稀糊狀，然後將菠菜落鍋拌合，即將火關熄。
4. 將湯倒入大碗中，撒下胡椒粉便可分食之。

Ingredients

150g. spinach,
1/2 box tender tofu,
1/2 cup sliced mushrooms
(or bamboo shoots),
100g. lean pork or 2 tbsp.
sliced ham (cooked),
6 cups soup stock

Seasonings

1 1/2 tsp. salt,
4 tbsp. cornstarch paste,
a punch of pepper

Procedures

1. Boil the spinach in boiling water over high heat for 5 seconds. Remove and rinse to cold immediately. Squeeze dry and chopped it into fine pieces.
2. Cut the bean curd into small cubes. Cook the lean pork until done then cut into small thin slices.
3. In a soup pot, bring 6 cups of soup stock to a boil. Add the mushrooms, pork, and tofu. When it boils again, thicken with cornstarch paste. Then add the spinach; stir until blended. Turn off the heat.
4. Pour the soup in a soup bowl. Sprinkle some black pepper on it and serve.

三鮮干絲湯

Chicken, Ham and Shrimp with Tofu Shreds Soup

材料 >>
白豆腐干（硬而薄者）300公克、蝦仁80公克、香菇絲1/3杯、熟雞絲1/2杯、火腿絲2大匙、清湯5杯

醃蝦仁料 >>
蛋白1/2大匙、太白粉1/2大匙

調味料 >>
鹽1茶匙

做法 >>
1. 將豆腐干切成與火柴棒相同之粗細絲狀後，全部用開水燙煮一次（約半分鐘）。
2. 干絲另加3杯清湯一起以小火煮約10分鐘，加鹽調味，盛入大碗中。
3. 蝦仁用醃蝦料拌過後，在開水內燙熟撈出。再與香菇絲，雞絲和火腿絲一起在2杯的清湯中煮一沸滾，即盛在大碗中干絲上面，即可上桌供食。

Ingredients
300g. dried white tofu (hard and thin),
80g. shelled small shrimp,
1/3 cup shredded black mushrooms,
1/2 cup shredded cooked chicken shreds,
2 tbsp. shredded ham,
5 cups soup

To marinate shrimp
1/2 tbsp. egg white,
1/2 tbsp. cornstarch

Seasonings
1 tsp. salt

Procedures
1. Cut the dried white tofu into fine shreds (match stick size). Boil them in boiling water for about 30 seconds. Remove and drain.
2. Cook the tofu shreds with 3 cups of soup stock over low heat for 10 minutes. Season with salt. Pour in a serving bowl.
3. Rinse the shrimp and mix with the marinades. Boil them in boiling water for a few seconds until done. Remove and drain. Cook the shrimp, mushrooms, chicken meat and ham in 2 cups of soup stock. Bring to a boil. Pour it over the tofu shreds and serve hot.

註 如無白豆腐乾,可將硬一點的豆腐整塊放在砧板上,上面再放重的物品,壓置約1小時左右,使豆腐中之多餘水份被壓擠出來、變硬實一些即可使用。

If you can not get the dried white tofu, you can use hard tofu instead. Put a chopping board and other heavy things on top of the tofu for about an hour. This will remove a lot of the moisture from the tofu. Then it can be cut into strips.

麵食篇

有關麵類

麵：有湯麵、炒麵及涼麵之別。

湯麵：又因所用主料與澆料之不同而名稱繁多，但原則上有3種方式做湯麵。其一是將澆料在鍋中做好之後，將麵條放進去同煮，煮至湯濃稠而鮮味透入麵中，北方俗稱"熱湯麵"，江浙人叫"煨麵"。其二者是將澆料做好澆到已盛在碗中之麵條上，如大滷麵、什錦麵、三鮮麵、牛肉麵等便是。第三種則係將已調味之清湯預先盛在碗內，將煮熟之麵條放進湯中，再在麵上擺上主料者，如排骨麵、雞腿麵、蹄花麵……等即是。

炒麵：其之種類也頗多，應注意事項為煮熟之麵條在炒前不可使其相黏（應沖過冷水，再拌少許熟油），炒時避免過於翻攪，以防麵條太爛、斷折。

涼麵：在夏天所常食，不但開胃，也有消暑之益，唯麵條煮熟後應使其冷透（沖過冰開水後瀝乾，或用電扇吹冷至涼透，再拌入植物油少許），拌涼麵之佐料及調味料應多備數種，以增加味道。

About Noodles

Noodles can be divided into major sections: noodle soup, fried noodles, and cold noodles. Noodle soup can also be divided into 3 sections:

1. Stir fry all of the ingredients and then add soup. When the soup is boiling, add the noodles and boil until the soup thickened and the noodles are done. Serve the noodles as they are with the soup.
2. Stir fry the ingredients and then put them on top of a bowl of noodle soup.
3. First, put some seasoned stock in a bowl. Then add the cooked noodles. On top of them, put the main ingredients.

In addition there are many kinds of stir-fried noodles. Fried noodles are first boiled before they are fried. Rinse cold to provent the noddles from sticking. Also you may mix with Aom oil before you stir-fry it.

Cold noodles are usually eaten in the summer. Boil the noodles until done. Then cool either by rinsing with cold water or using a fan. Add a little vegetable oil. Finally, add the other ingredients and seasonings. Mix well and serve.

菜包子
Steamed Pastries with Vegetables

材料 >>
麵粉3 1/2杯、白糖1大匙、酵母粉2茶匙、溫水1 1/2杯、發泡粉2茶匙、冷水1/2大匙、青江菜或高麗菜600公克、香菇屑3大匙、蔥屑1大匙

調味料 >>
鹽2茶匙、麻油1大匙、醬油1大匙

註　此種菜包內也可加入泡軟之粉絲（切短）及豆腐干、油豆腐、洋菇、木耳之類材料。

The recipe for Meat Pastry is on page 247 of Vol. I Pei Mei's Chinese Cook Book.

做法 >>

1. 將酵母粉放在溫水中溶化，倒入盛在盆內之麵粉中（糖已拌在麵粉內），調拌均勻、用手揉合成一糰，上面覆蓋一塊微濕之布，放置一旁，使其發酵（時間長短需視氣候而定，通常3、4小時足夠）。
2. 青江菜洗淨、切碎，撒上鹽（1茶匙）拌醃，約20分鐘後擠去水份，再加以剁碎，盛在大碗內。加入香菇屑（也需剁得極碎）、蔥屑與調味料拌勻。
3. 將發酵好之麵糰移到麵板上，加入用水溶化之發泡粉後加以揉光。搓成長條，再分切成雞蛋大小之小塊，然後將每一塊用擀麵杖擀成厚約0.5公分之圓形麵皮。
4. 將菜餡酌量放進麵皮中間，並用手將麵皮外沿提起，周圍用拇指和食指順序做成許多小摺子，直至最後摺子接合在中間收緊，便算包好。
5. 包子放置20分鐘，見略似發醒狀，即排入蒸籠中，上鍋用大火蒸約20分鐘便成。

Ingredients

3 1/2 cups flour,
1 tbsp. sugar,
2 tsp. dried yeast,
1 1/2 cups warm water,
2 tsp. baking powder,
1/2 tbsp. cold water,
600g. green cabbage,
3 tbsp. chopped black mushroom,
1 tbsp. chopped green onion

Seasonings

2 tsp. salt,
1 tsp. sesame oil,
1 tbsp. soy sauce

Procedures

1. Mix the flour and sugar in a large bowl. Dissolve the dried yeast in warm water (about 40°C). Add to the bowl, knead into a dough. Cover the dough with a wet cloth and let it rise. (the time for rising varies according to the temperature, usually about 3 to 4 hours is enough). After risen, add baking powder (dissolve in 1/2 tbsp. cold water first) and knead again.
2. Dice the cabbage; mix the cabbage with 1 tbsp. salt for 20 minutes. Then squeeze it dry and chop it finely. Put it into a bowl, mix with chopped green onion, finely chopped black mushrooms and seasonings. This is the stuffing.
3. Knead the dough on a pastry board again. Then cut into small pieces about the size of an egg. Flatten the small dough with the palm and roll out with a rolling pin. Make each one into a round cake about 0.5 cm thick. This is the wrapper.
4. Put about 1 1/2 tbsp. stuffings on the center of one wrapper. Pleat the wrapper and center all the pleats to the top with a twist. Make sure the wrapper is closed tightly.
5. Let the shaped dumplings rest for 20 minutes. Then place on a wet cloth on a steamer. Steam over boiling water for about 20 minutes.

麵食篇
培梅食譜 II

花捲
Steamed Flower Shaped Rolls

材料 >>

麵粉3 1/2杯、酵母粉2茶匙、溫水1 1/2杯、發泡粉2茶匙、冷水1/2大匙

調味料 >>

油1/3杯、鹽1茶匙

做法 >>

1. 將酵母粉放在溫水中溶化後，倒入盛在盆內的麵粉中調拌，並用手揉合成一麵糰，上面覆蓋乾淨之濕布，放置一旁使其發酵（時間長、短，需視氣候而定，普通室內溫度約2至3小時便可發起）。
2. 約數小時後，見麵糰已膨脹而內部成蜂巢狀時，便可全部由盆中取出，並加入用水1/2大匙調溶之發泡粉一起放在麵板上，再用力揉搓約5分鐘，使麵糰變成光滑而柔軟。
3. 然後先搓揉成粗條，再用擀麵棍擀成四方形薄餅，再平均刷上一層油及撒上少許鹽，便捲成長筒狀，用刀切成約6公分長小段，再用竹筷順著切斷面的方向，在當中壓3～4道深痕。
4. 放置15分鐘左右，稍見發鬆後，始可裝進蒸籠中，用大火蒸20分鐘（鍋中之水沸滾後才可以放上蒸籠去蒸）。

Ingredients

3 1/2 cups flour (all purpose),
2 tsp. dried yeast,
1 1/2 cups warm water,
2 tsp. baking powder,
1/2 tbsp. cold water

Seasonings

1/3 cup oil,
1 tsp. salt

Procedures

1. Dissolve the yeast in warm water. Add to flour and knead until smooth. Cover with damp cloth. Let it rise for about 2 to 3 hours.
2. When the dough has risen, add the baking powder (dissolved in 1/2 tbsp. cold water first). Knead again for about 5 minutes, knead until smooth and elastic.
3. Roll out the dough into a thin square. Sprinkle lightly with oil and salt. Roll the dough up tightly as for a jelly roll. Cut into 6 cm sections. Using a chopstick, press down 3~4 times on the top of each piece.
4. Let the rolls rest for 15 minutes. Then place on a wet cloth on a steamer. Steam over boiling water for about 20 minutes over high heat.

 花捲之形狀各式各種非常繁多、美觀，可任意創造試捲之。

Many different shapes of this roll may be made. You don't have to make it the exact way which mentioned above. Use your imagination to think of a new shape.

材料 >>

餡料：紅燒肉1杯、蝦米2大匙、香菇3朵、糯米飯3杯

外皮：中筋麵粉3杯、開水1杯、冷水1/4杯

調味料 >>

醬油2大匙、豬油1大匙、胡椒粉1/4茶匙

做法 >>

1. 將麵粉量置在盆內，沖下開水，並用筷子拌勻，再將冷水放入，用手揉合搓成硬度適中之麵糰（此種麵糰應較普通所用的硬一點），蓋上一塊濕布，放置15分鐘以上。
2. 將紅燒肉、泡軟之蝦米和香菇分別剁爛，放在大碗內待用。
3. 糯米飯趁熱用筷子撥散，放入大碗內，和第2項之各料及調味料混合，用手仔細攪拌均勻成為餡料。
4. 將第一項之麵糰移到麵板上，再加揉搓一次，並分成30小粒，每粒用擀麵杖擀成5公分直徑之圓形薄餅皮。在中間放進1 1/2大匙餡料，用大拇指與2拇指將麵皮從中腰處捏緊，使餡料裹在內部、而呈花瓶狀之燒賣。
5. 將做好之燒賣全部排放到蒸籠內，上鍋大火蒸15分鐘便成。

Ingredients

For filling: 1 cup stewed pork, 2 tbsp. dried shrimp, 3 black mushrooms, 3 cups cooked glutinous rice

For wrapper: 3 cups flour, 1 cup boiling water, 1/4 cup cold water (or less)

Seasonings

2 tbsp. soy sauce, 1 tbsp. lard or oil, 1/4 tsp. black pepper

Procedures

1. Place flour in a large bowl. Add boiling water and mix well. Add suitable amount of cold water; knead the dough with hands until thoroughly mixed. Cover and let it set for at least 15 minutes.
2. Chop the stewed pork, soaked dried shrimp, and soaked mushrooms finely. Place into a bowl.
3. Add the cooked glutinous rice to No. 2 bowl; also add seasonings; mix will with your hands or chopsticks until they are thoroughly combined—this is the filling.
4. Remove the dough and knead again; cut into 30 pieces. Flatten each small dough with your hand and roll it out to about 5cm round (this is the wrapper) .Place the wrapper on your palm and put 1 1/2 tbsp. filling on it. With your fingers gather up, pinch and pleat the wrapper around the filling to from an open-topped pouch. Pinch the top gently in the middle to give it a waist. (like a flower vase).
5. Arrange the dumplings in a steamer, steam over high heat for about 15 minutes. Remove to a plate to serve.

糯米燒賣
Stewed Pork and Glutinous Rice Dumplings

註 紅燒肉做法：請參照培梅食譜第一冊176頁"紅燜肉"即可。

The recipe for stewed pork can be found on page 176 of Pei Mei's Chinese Cook Book Vol. I.

燒餅
Baked Sesame Seed Buns

材料 >>
中筋麵粉600公克（約5杯）、開水1 1/2杯、冷水2/3杯至1杯、鹽1 1/2茶匙、白芝麻3大匙

調味料 >>
麵粉1杯、油2/3杯

做法 >>

1. 油酥做法：鍋內放油2/3杯，待油熱後加入麵粉1杯，不停的炒拌、攪動，約5分鐘後，盛在小鋁盆內，放入烤箱中用120℃、烘約30分鐘，至顏色轉為茶黃色且有香氣為止（冷後使用）。也可用極小的火候在爐子上炒約10分鐘左右至成茶黃也可。

2. 將麵粉盛在大盆內，沖下開水1 1/2杯，並用筷子快速調拌，1分鐘後將2/3杯冷水慢慢加入，並用手揉至光滑成為麵糰，放置20分鐘左右。

3. 將麵糰放在麵板上再揉一次。用擀麵杖推擀成0.4公分厚的四方大麵片，然後把油酥塗抹在大麵片上，並撒上鹽（需很均勻）。把麵片從手邊向前捲起，使其成為筒狀。用手（或刀）將麵筒分成20個小塊。

4. 把小麵塊橫放在麵板上（切口向左右放），從中間一半的地方向前推擀，然後捲蓋起來，再從中間一半處往前再推擀壓扁，再捲蓋起來。翻一個面並換個邊（切口兩端向著前後），從中間一半處又往前推擀並相疊起來，再翻一面，從一半處又向前推擀一次之後，用手捲起成為捲筒狀。（共計推擀了4次、捲蓋4次）。

5. 將捲筒狀之麵塊，在光滑之一面上，沾上芝麻，放置約5分鐘。再用擀麵棍先擀好寬度（約5公分）再加以擀長（約10公分）。

6. 將芝麻面向下，排列在烤盤內，放入已燒至180℃之烤箱內，烤至麵餅上面鼓起。拉出烤盤，將燒餅翻一個面再烤，至呈金黃色為止，即成燒餅。

Ingredients

5 cups flour,
1 1/2 cups boiling water,
2/3 cup cold water,
1 1/2 tsp. salt,
3 tbsp. sesame seeds

Oiled flour

1 cup flour,
2/3 cup oil

 燒餅除可夾油條之外，也可夾蛋餅、蒙古烤肉或蔥爆肉之類的菜式而食。

This sesame seed bun can be opened and a yu-tiao or Mangolian Bar. B.Q pork or stir fry egg can be placed in it.

Procedures

1. For oiled flour: Heat 2/3 cup of oil in a pan and add 1 cup of flour. Stir fry over low heat for about 5 minutes. Put the mixture in a bowl and bake in an oven over 120°C (about 300°F) for 30 minutes until the mixture turns golden brown and smells good. Then let the mixture cool. (or you can stir fry the mixture over very low heat for 10 minutes until it is golden brown).

2. Place 5 cups of flour in a bowl. Add the boiling water. Mix with chopsticks thoroughly then add cold water; knead into a dough. Let it stand for at least 20 minutes.

3. Remove the dough to a board and knead it again. Then roll the dough out into a 0.4 cm thin square. Pour the oiled flour on top; spread evenly over the dough. Sprinkle the top with salt. Roll the dough up like a jelly roll, and then divide it into 20 small pieces.

4. Put one piece of the dough on the board (cutting side on right and left). Roll out from the center to the front and then fold over. Repeat this procedure. Then turn the dough over and change the side (the cutting sides on the front and back) and repeat the rolling procedure. Then turn the dough over and repeat the rolling procedure once more. Roll it up at last.

5. Dip the smooth surface into the sesame seeds. Let it stand for about 5 minutes. Roll out the dough to about 10 cm long and 5 cm wide.

6. Preheat the oven to 180°C, bake the dough for about 5 minutes (with the sesame seeds side down). Bake until the top is pop up and becomes golden brown; turn the dough over and bake for another 5 minutes.

油條
You-Tiao

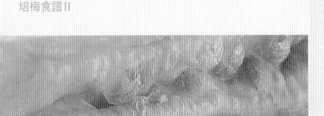

材料 >> （室溫攝氏20度時）
高筋麵粉600公克（約5杯）、阿摩尼亞粉（氨粉）11公克（約2 1/2茶匙）、小蘇打粉9公克（1 1/2茶匙）、明礬5.5公克（1 1/2茶匙）、鹽1 1/2茶匙、水1 1/2杯至2杯（約450CC）、炸油10杯

做法 >>

1. 在一只清潔的盆中，將阿摩尼亞粉、小蘇打粉、明礬、鹽等原料量好，然後倒下水1 1/2杯使其溶解（沖下水時會有白泡沫及聲音產生）。

2. 將麵粉全部倒入盆中與所有原料相混合，並用手揉搓，使成為一塊麵糰，然後握緊拳頭、沾水少許，揣壓麵糰，由中間往四週壓，再將麵邊拉扯回中間覆蓋，再壓、再蓋，重覆約5分鐘，用一塊濕布蓋在盆上，放置一旁。

3. 約30分鐘後再揣壓一次麵糰（約十數下），然後再放置使其醒發。

4. 再過30分鐘，重再揣麵一次，並在表面上塗少許油（預防表面乾硬），用一大張塑膠紙包捲成一長枕頭狀放置。

5. 約4～5小時後（時間之長短視氣溫之高低而不同）即將麵糰倒在麵板上，輕輕拉長，不可揉搓，擀平成為8公分寬、0.6公分厚之長片（厚薄需平均），然後用刀切成1.5公分寬之小條，將每兩小條正面相對合的疊成一組，用細竹筷在中間直條、用力的壓一道溝，再用雙手手指上下捏住兩端，先拉長（約45公分長）再迅速由鍋邊滑入沸油鍋中，大火炸熟至呈金黃色又酥脆便可（炸時需用竹筷不停的翻動），趁熱食之極為香酥可口。

Ingredients

(when the room temperature is about 20.C)

600g. flour (all purpose),
11g. powdered ammonia (about 2 1/2 tsp.),
9g. baking soda (1 1/2 tsp.),
5.5g. alum (1 1/2 tsp.),
1 1/2 tsp. salt,
1 1/2 cups water,
10 cups oil

 做油條用的配料的份量（阿摩尼亞、小蘇打和明礬）天冷需減少，天熱需增加，每10°C增減20%為標準。

For this recipe, the room temperature should be about 70°F (20°C). If the temperature is 20°F (10°C) lower, reduce the ammonia, alum, and baking soda for about 20%.

Procedures

1. In a clean bowl, measure and add the ammonia powder, baking soda , alum, and salt. Then add 1 1/2 cup of water. Mix well. (when mixing these ingredients will create bubbles and a little noise).
2. Add the flour and mix well. Knead the mixture with your fist. If it sticks to your hands, dip some water on hands and continue to knead for 5 minutes. Cover with a wet cloth and set aside.
3. After 30 minutes, knead the dough again. Then set it aside again.
4. After 30 minutes, knead the dough again into a pillow shape. Rub a little of cooking oil on the surface so that the dough won't dry out. Wrap the dough in plastic paper and put it in a warm place.
5. Set aside for 4~5 hours depending on the temperature (if it is hot, 4 hours will be enough). Put the dough on a floured broad. Lightly draw the dough. Don't knead it. Flatten the dough into a long piece about 8cm wide and 0.6cm thick. Use a knife to cut it into 1.5cm wide pieces. Pick up one strip of dough and turn it upside down on another strip. Use a thin chopstick to make a small, long dent length wise. Pick up with the two end of the strip and pull it until it is about 45 cm long. Quickly slip the strip into very hot oil. Use chopsticks to turn theYou-tiao continuously until it is golden brown. Eat them while they are hot.

廣州燴飯
Rice with Assorted Ingredients, Cantonese Style

材料 >> （4人份）
蝦仁20隻、新鮮魷魚1條、叉燒肉80公克、草菇12個、筍1支、芥蘭菜（4公分長）12支、蔥段10小支、清湯4杯、白米飯4碗

調味料 >>
醬油2大匙、鹽2/3茶匙、糖1/4茶匙、太白粉水2大匙、麻油1/2茶匙

Ingredients (To serve 4)

20 small shelled shrimps,
1 squid or cuttlefish,
80g. roast pork (or ham),
12 straw mushrooms,
1 bamboo shoot,
12 Chinese broccoli (4cm long),
10 pieces green onion (3 cm long),
4 cups soup stock,
6 cups cooked rice (hot)

Seasonings

2 tbsp. soy sauce,
2/3 tsp. salt,
1/4 tsp. sugar,
2 tbsp. cornstarch paste,
1/2 tbsp. sesame oil

Procedures

1. Rinse the shrimps, pat it dry and then mix with 1 tsp. cornstarch. Score the inside of the squid, then cut into small pieces. Slice the roasted pork into thin slices. Cut each mushroom into halves. Cook the bamboo shoot, and then slice it.
2. Boil the shrimp, squid, and broccoli in boiling water for about 5 seconds (add some wine into the boiling water first). Remove and drain.
3. Heat 3 tbsp. oil in a pan. Stir fry green onion, mushrooms and bamboo shoot. Add soup stock, soy sauce, salt and sugar. When the soup is boiling, add the boiled ingredients of No. 2 and the roast pork slices. Thicken the soup with cornstarch paste. Turn off the heat. Splash sesame oil on it. Serve the cooked rice on individual plates, and pour the assorted ingredients sauce over the rice.

 燴飯所用之材料種類與份量可按個人喜愛及方便，多少可隨意增減。
This dish is usually made according to the cook's individual taste. You may use any other ingredients you like.

做法 >>

1. 蝦仁洗淨,用太白粉1茶匙調拌;魷魚在內部切交叉刀紋,再分割成小塊;叉燒肉切成片;草菇一切為二;筍煮熟、切片。
2. 燒開一鍋滾水、淋下酒後,投下蝦仁,鮮魷魚片和芥蘭菜等,川燙5秒鐘即全部撈出。
3. 起油鍋,先爆香蔥段,再炒草菇和筍片,注入清湯,加入醬油,鹽,糖調味後,將上項燙過之材料及叉燒肉落鍋,並馬上用太白粉水勾芡,熄火後淋下麻油,分別澆到盛在碟內的白飯上即可。

翡翠炒飯
Fried Rice with Green Vegetables

材料 >>
青江菜300公克、火腿（或鹹肉，香腸也可）80公克、蛋1個、蔥屑2大匙、白米飯4碗

調味料 >>
鹽2茶匙

做法 >>

1. 將青江菜洗淨、切碎,撒下1茶匙的鹽拌醃。約十數分鐘後,將水份擠乾,再用刀斬剁成小碎粒狀。(愈碎愈好)。
2. 蛋打散、鍋中塗少許油,做成蛋皮,切成小丁;火腿(先蒸熟)也切成小丁。
3. 用1大匙油在鍋內燒熱,放下青江菜,以大火炒熟(約20～30秒鐘),盛出。
4. 另將炒鍋燒熱,放下油2大匙,待油熱後落蔥屑下鍋爆香,再倒下米飯,待炒透後加鹽調味,並將青江菜及蛋丁、火腿丁等也放下一起拌炒,炒至十分乾鬆、均勻時便可裝盤上桌。翠綠可愛,風味另幟。

Ingredients

300g. green cabbage,
80g. ham or roasted pork,
1 egg,
2 tbsp. chopped green onion,
4 cups cooked rice

Seasonings

2 tsp. salt

Procedures

1. Rinse the cabbage and cut it into shreds. Pickle the cabbage with 1 tsp. salt for about 10 minutes. Then squeeze dry and chop it finely.
2. Heat a little of oil in a frying pan. Pour in the beaten egg, make a thin egg pancake. Remove the egg pancake and dice it into small pieces. Also dice ham for later use.
3. Heat 1 tbsp. oil in a pan. Stir fry the cabbage for about 20~30 seconds and remove from the pan.
4. Heat another 2 tbsp. oil in the same pan. Fry the chopped green onion for about 5 seconds. Then put in the rice and stir fry until heated. Season with salt, then add cabbage, egg, and ham. Stir well and serve.

山東大滷麵
Assorted Meat in soup Noodles

註 花椒油做法：將乾淨的油1/2杯燒熱，放下1大匙花椒粒，小火炸到花椒變黑時，撈出花椒，而該油即是花椒油，可裝進小瓶內留用。

To make brown pepper corn oil : Fry 1 tbsp. brown pepper corn with 1/2 cup of oil, fry until they turn black, discard the pepper corn and keep this oil in a small bottle.

材料 >> （4碗份）

熟豬肉片1杯、海參1條、蝦仁20隻、木耳（泡發）1/2杯、黃瓜片（或小白菜）1/2杯、蛋2個、細麵條500公克、清湯6杯

調味料 >>

醬油3大匙、鹽1茶匙、太白粉水3大匙、麻油1/2大匙、花椒油1/2大匙

做法 >>

1. 蝦仁在背部切劃一條刀口；海參先用水（加酒少許）煮5～10分鐘除去腥味後切斜片留用。
2. 將清湯煮滾，放下肉片、木耳、海參、蝦仁及黃瓜片，並放醬油和鹽調味。待再度煮滾時，淋下用水調濕之太白粉水勾芡成稀糊狀。
3. 將火改小淋下打散之蛋汁，慢慢攪勻，待蛋絲凝結浮到湯面時將火關熄。滴下麻油與花椒油。
4. 在一大鍋滾水中將麵條煮熟，撈出1/4量到一只碗內，澆上約1 1/2杯量之第3項滷料，即成為一份大滷麵。

Ingredients
(To serve 4)

1 cup of cooked pork slices,
1 sea cucumber,
20 small shrimp,
1/2 cup soaked fungus,
1/2 cup cucumber slices (or other green vegetables),
2 eggs,
500g. fresh noodles,
6 cups of soup stock

Seasonings

3 tbsp. soy sauce,
1 tsp. salt,
3 tbsp. cornstarch paste,
1/2 tbsp. sesame oil,
1/2 tbsp. brown pepper corn oil

Procedures

1. De-vein the shrimp and make a score on the back; rinse and drain. Put sea cucumber in cold water with some wine; bring to a boil, cook over low heat for about 5~10 minutes. Remove and cut into slices.
2. Boil the soup stock in a sauce pan. Add pork, fungus, sea cucumber, shrimp and cucumber slices. Season with soy sauce and salt. When it boils again, thicken with cornstarch paste.
3. Reduce the heat. Pour in the beaten egg carefully and stir until blended. Turn off the heat. Splash sesame oil and brown pepper corn oil on top.
4. Cook the noodles in boiling water. When it is cooked, remove to 4 bowls. Pour 1 1/2 cups of the sauce over the noodles and serve immediately.

北方炸醬麵
Noodles with Minced Pork and Bean Sauce

材料 >>（5碗份）

新鮮麵條500公克、絞豬肉（半肥瘦）300公克、大白菜150公克、蝦米2大匙、毛豆2大匙、蔥屑3大匙、黃瓜1條 或綠豆芽1杯、蛋2個、胡蘿蔔絲1/2杯、清湯或水1/2杯

調味料 >>

鹽1茶匙、甜麵醬5大匙、醬油2大匙、薑汁1/2大匙、糖1/2茶匙、麻油1茶匙

做法 >>

1. 將大白菜全部切成如紅豆般大小之粒狀；蝦米泡軟後略加切碎備用。
2. 甜麵醬盛在碗內，加入醬油、薑汁、糖和麻油調勻。
3. 起油鍋先用4大匙油炒豬肉及蝦米，約半分鐘後，再加入白菜丁，並注入清水1/2杯，放下毛豆及鹽後，蓋上鍋蓋煮約1分鐘全部盛出。
4. 另燒熱2大匙油爆炒蔥屑，隨即將調拌過之甜麵醬傾下鍋中，用小火炒香，再將第3項之材料落鍋，大火炒拌均勻便可盛入深碟子中。
5. 將麵條煮熟後撈出，沖過冷開水再瀝乾，分別盛在碗中上桌。食時放上2大匙炸醬及少許黃瓜絲、蛋皮絲或綠豆芽、胡蘿蔔絲等，應多加調拌均勻。

Ingredients (To serve 4)

500g. fresh noodles,
300g. ground pork (or beef),
150g. chinese cabbage,
2 tbsp. dried shrimp,
2 tbsp. fresh soybeans (or green peas),
3 tbsp. chopped green onion,
1/2 cup shredded cucumber (or bean sprouts),
2 eggs,
1/2 cup carrot shreds,
1/2 cup soup stock or water

Seasonings

1 tsp. salt,
5 tbsp. soybean paste,
2 tbsp. soy sauce,
1/2 tbsp. ginger juice,
1/2 tsp. sugar,
1 tsp. sesame oil

Procedures

1. Cut the cabbage into small cubes; Soak the dried shrimp in warm water for about 10 minutes. Chop it finely.
2. Combine the soy bean paste, soy sauce, sugar, ginger juice, and sesame oil. Mix thoroughly.
3. Heat 4 tbsp. oil to stir fry ground pork and dried shrimp. After 1/2 minute, add the cabbage, soy beans, soup stock and salt. Cover and cook for 1 minute over low heat. Remove.
4. Heat 2 tbsp. oil to stir fry the green onion for a while, add soy bean paste, stir fry until fragrant. Add meat mixture; stir fry over high heat for 1 minute. Remove to a bowl.
5. Boil the noodles in boiling water until done. (If you use fresh Chinese thin noodles, 2 minutes is enough). Remove the cooked noodles and plunge into cold water, and then drain. Serve the noodles in individual bowls. At the table, put l or 2 tbsp. meat sauce on top of the noodles. Mix thoroughly with chopsticks before eating. (Some shredded cucumbers, shredded carrot, shredded egg sheets or scrambled eggs and cooked bean sprouts can be added with these noodles).

川味涼麵
Cold Noodles, Sichuan Style

材料 >>
熟雞絲1杯、綠豆芽2杯、細麵條500公克、沙拉油2大匙、麻油1大匙、碎花生屑（炒過的）1大匙

調味料 >>
芝麻醬3大匙、醬油6大匙、醋1大匙、糖1茶匙、蔥屑2大匙、薑汁1/2大匙、蒜泥1/2大匙、花椒粉1/2茶匙、辣椒油1大匙、麻油1大匙

1. 這種四川式涼麵因所用調味料及辛香料多，味道特殊而可口。
2. 麵條如果是現吃而不久放時，也可在煮好之後，馬上泡過冰開水，再加以瀝乾就淋上佐料拌食。

1. This is a very famous Sichuan style noodles, it is very tasteful since we use a lot of spices and condiments to make the sauce.
2. You may just rinse the noodles to cold instead of mix with oil, if you prepare to eat it right after you make it.

做法 >>

1. 將麵條下鍋用開水煮熟後撈出（需瀝乾水份），放在一個大盤子上，淋下1大匙麻油，而盤子上也需預先刷上2大匙沙拉油或麻油，再馬上用筷子挑起麵條，用電風扇吹涼（要頻頻拉高麵條，使麵不要黏連才好）。
2. 用開水燙煮綠豆芽約10秒鐘，撈出後沖過冰開水，使其冷透並擠乾水份，放在大盤子中做底，上面放已吹冷之涼麵，再將雞肉絲（煮熟之雞肉切成3～4公分長絲狀），擺在麵條上。
3. 用一只碗，調勻芝麻醬與醬油（醬油應1大匙、1大匙的加入，每加一次需調拌均勻），然後加入醋等調味料拌合，澆到雞絲涼麵上，再撒下花生米屑上桌，食時再加以仔細拌勻即可。

Ingredients

1 cup chicken meat (cooked and shredded),
2 cups bean sprouts,
500g. fresh noodles,
2 tbsp. oil,
1 tbsp. sesame oil,
1 tbsp. chopped peanuts (roasted)

Seasonings sauce

3 tbsp. sesame seed paste,
6 tbsp. soy sauce,
1 tbsp. vinegar,
1 tsp. sugar,
2 tbsp. chopped green onion,
1/2 tbsp. ginger juice,
1/2 tbsp. smashed garlic,
1/2 tsp. brown pepper corm powder,
1 tbsp. hot red chili oil,
1 tbsp. sesame oil

Procedures

1. Cook the noodles in boiling water until the water boils again. Then add 1/2 cup of cold water and bring to a boil again. Remove the noodles immediately when it is done. Put it on a platter which has 2 tbsp. oil on it; add another 1 tbsp. sesame oil to noodles. Then use chopsticks to stir the noodles and use a fan to cool the noodles at the same time. This is to prevent the noodles from sticking together.
2. Boil the bean sprouts in boiling water for 10 seconds. Then remove and plunge into cold water; squeeze it dry, put on a serving platter and place the noodles over it. Then put the chicken on the noodles.
3. Mix the sesame seed paste with 1 tbsp. soy sauce in a small bowl. Mixed thoroughly; then add another tbsp. soy sauce, mix well. Repeat this procedure until all the 6 tbsp. soy sauce have been used up. Then add the other seasonings to make the seasonings sauce. Pour the sauce over the noodles. Sprinkle chopped peanuts over it. Mix well just before eating.

甜 點 篇

有關甜點類

　　做中式甜點所用之材料，除麵粉、糖、油、蛋等之外，尚有許多種是使用糯米或糯米粉，以及用豆沙做餡心者。而中式甜點多以蒸熟，或炸脆，或烤黃，或烘酥為完成方式。

　　甜點所用之麵粉應以中筋或低筋為宜，尤其發酵後再製做之糕餅、包子類，切忌使用高筋麵粉。為了使做好之糕包類光亮、平滑起見，可在發酵完成後酌加快速發粉（即 baking Powder）。

　　甜湯之製作目前為求迅速，無論湯、露、糊、羹均採取煮的方法，羹與糊則需使用澱粉料（如玉米粉或上好太白粉）勾芡，使湯呈稠濃狀，適宜在冷天食用。

　　甜湯中所放糖的份量不可過多、以免太膩。

About Desserts

　　Chinese desserts, in addition to the traditional ingredients of flour, sugar, oil and eggs, also glutinous rice or powder and red bean paste which is used as a filling are often used. These desserts are often steamed, deep fried, baked, or roasted.

　　Most sweet desserts use cake flour. If one uses yeast for cakes or bread, one should avoid using all purpose flour. To make cakes and bread bright and smooth, add a little baking powder to the already risen dough.

　　Sweet soups can be quickly prepared by using boiling method. Usually they are just with a potage or cream soup, a cornstarch paste must be used to thicken the liquid. These are especially suitable in cold weather. Don't add additional sugar to the served sweet soup may make it too sweet.

壽桃

Steamed Long Life Cake

材料 >>

麵粉 3 1/2 杯、酵母粉 2 茶匙、溫水 1 1/2 杯、豬油 3 大匙、白糖 3 大匙、豆沙 300 公克、發泡粉 2 茶匙

做法 >>

1 將酵母粉傾入溫水中泡約 2 分鐘，使其溶解。在大盆中放入麵粉並加豬油與糖拌合，然後將已溶解之酵母粉水倒下，用手拌合，並揉成軟度適中之麵糰，在上面覆蓋一塊微濕之白布，放置一旁待其發酵（約 3 小時）。

2 在已發好之麵糰內加入發泡粉 2 茶匙（需用水 1/2 大匙先加以溶化），再移到麵板上，重加揉搓至十分光滑為止（約 5 分鐘）。

3 將麵糰分成 10 小塊，每小塊用手掌先略加揉圓之後壓扁一些，放進一小球豆沙餡包合起來並收緊，再倒轉一頭，放到手掌中，用兩個手掌之邊緣搓弄出一個尖角來，放回麵板上。用小刀順著尖角方向劃切一道深溝，並使尖角更尖銳些。在每一個壽桃下面放一小張白紙。

4 全部做好、放在麵板上醒發（約 30 分鐘），然後排列到蒸籠內，水滾之後上鍋，用大火蒸約 20 分鐘左右即熟。

Ingredients

3 1/2 cups flour, 2 tsp. dried yeast, 1 1/2 cups warm water, 3 tsp. lard, 3 tbsp. sugar, 300g. sweet red bean paste, 2 tsp. baking powder

Procedures

1 Dissolve the dried yeast in warm water for about 2 minutes. Add to flour in a large bowl with lard and sugar. Knead with hands until very smooth. Cover with a piece of wet cloth. Let stand and rise for about 3 hours.

2 When the dough has risen, add the baking powder (dissolve with 1/2 tbsp. cold water). Knead again. Remove to light floured board. Knead a few minutes more until smooth.

3 Divide the dough into 10 even pieces. Knead and roll each piece of dough into 7cm in diameter. Place a little of sweet bean paste (size of a walnut) in the center, pinch and pleat dough around all the edges up to top center. Seal tightly and then turn it over. Roll the dough between your palms until you make a sharp point on the top. Then use a knife to cut a slit from the point to the bottom on one side.

4 Place a small piece of white paper under each cake. Let it rest for 30 minutes. Then place all of them in a steamer and steam for about 20 minutes over high heat.

註 壽桃多在慶生筵上做甜點之用，為求美觀，通常附加2枚葉子在下部左右方，形似真桃子更加美觀。

These cakes are served on birthdays since they represent long life. This cake is about the same shape as a peach. To decorate the cakes, you can add a little green food coloring to some of the risen dough, then add to the sides to make leaves. Finally, steam the cake with its leaves.

花生糊
Sweet Peanut Cream Soup

材料 >>
花生醬（甜）6大匙、紅棗6粒、水6杯

調味料 >>
糖8大匙、太白粉水5大匙

做法 >>
1 將花生醬放在大碗中，先加入半杯水慢慢調勻，不可有顆粒狀，然後再加入另外半杯水，邊加邊攪，總共用兩杯水調稀即可備煮。
2 將餘下的 4 杯水盛在鍋中，用小火煮滾，加糖後隨即將上項調好之花生醬倒下攪勻，待再沸滾時，淋下調水之太白粉慢慢勾芡，煮成糊狀，倒入大碗內。
3 紅棗泡 1 小時後去核，將棗肉切成碎屑，撒在花生糊面上即可上桌。（此種甜湯也可加入牛奶水或鮮奶油 3 大匙攪勻供食，風味更佳）。

Ingredients
6 tbsp. sweet peanut butter,
6 red dates,
6 cups water

Seasonings
8 tbsp. sugar,
5 tbsp. cornstarch paste

Procedures
1 Mix the 6 tbsp. peanut butter with 1/2 cup of water in a bowl until well mixed. Then add an additional 1/2 cup of water. Mix well. Repeat this procedure until the 2 cups of water have been used up.
2 Put the other 4 cups of water and 8 tbsp. sugar into a pot. Bring it to a boil. Then add the peanut paste; mix thoroughly until it boils again. Thicken it with cornstarch paste. Pour it to a large serving bowl.
3 Soak the red dates in warm water for about one hour. Remove the seeds and dice the pulp finely. Then sprinkle over the peanut cream soup and serve.

 此種甜糊也可加入牛奶水 3 大匙攪勻供食，風味更佳。
This soup tastes much better if you add 3 tbsp. fresh cream or condensed milk before adding the dates.

豆沙芋棗
Fried Taro Dumplings with Sweet Bean Paste

材料 >>
大芋頭600公克、蓮藕粉1杯（或玉米粉）、開水1/2杯、豆沙250公克、太白粉1/2杯

調味料 >>
豬油3大匙、糖4大匙

Ingredients
600g. taro (or potato),
1 cup lotus root starch (or cornstarch),
1/2 cup boiling water,
250g. sweet bean paste,
1/2 cup cornstarch

Seasonings
3 tbsp. lard,
4 tbsp. sugar

Procedures
1. After peeling the skin off from the taro, cut it into thin slices. Place in a steamer; steam for about 20 minutes until done. Remove the taro and mash it while it is warm (don't use the hard part).
2. Pour the boiling water into the lotus root starch. Stir well until it is half done; mix with the mashed taro; add the lard and sugar; knead the taro mixture until smooth. Let it stand for 10 minutes.
3. Divide the sweet bean paste into 30 small pieces. Roll each with palm. Place on a plate for later use.
4. Divide the taro mixture into 30 small pieces. Roll each piece into a ball. Put one piece of red bean paste into the center of the taro ball. Seal the edge and roll it into an oval shape.
5. Coat all the taro balls with cornstarch. Deep fry it in warm oil for about 2 minutes until crisp. Remove and serve.

做法 >>

1. 大芋頭去皮後切成大片，放在蒸籠內蒸20分鐘，蒸熟後取出，趁熱用刀面壓碎（壓不碎的部份不用）。
2. 將開水沖入蓮藕粉中、使藕粉成半熟狀後，放進芋頭中，再加入豬油及糖，仔細用手搓勻，揉成一糰，放置10分鐘。
3. 豆沙分成30小粒，每粒用手掌搓成圓球狀備用。
4. 將芋頭糰分成30小塊，每一小塊用手掌搓圓，並在中間包入豆沙一小球，捏住封口後，再搓成枕頭形（即棗子形）。
5. 全部做好後滾上乾太白粉，投入溫油中用小火炸至鬆酥即成（約2分鐘）。

八寶芋泥
Steamed Eight Treasures Taro Pudding

材料 >>
大芋頭900公克、糖漿2/3杯、豬油3大匙、乾蓮子20粒、葡萄乾20粒、紅棗8個、冬瓜糖4條、橘子餅2個、青、紅絲隨意

做法 >>
1. 選購花紋較多的大芋頭，削皮後切成大薄片，放在蒸籠內、蒸約 20 分鐘至軟爛（可用筷子試插、容易插透便可）。
2. 紅棗用水泡軟（約 1 小時），每個切成 4 片，中心之核籽去掉；乾蓮子泡 3 小時至漲大；桔餅切成小粒；冬瓜糖也切粒備用。
3. 用一只大碗或模型，在內面塗滿一層豬油（約 1 大匙），然後將上項各料分別排入成為圖案。
4. 將蒸爛之芋頭趁熱用刀子將它壓成泥狀（須很細勻才好），放入碗內，並加進糖漿及 2 大匙豬油攪拌均勻，然後填入做法 3 之大碗中，上面蓋一個碟子，上鍋蒸約 1 小時，端出後扣覆在大盤內，即可上桌。

Ingredients

900g. taro,
2/3 cup light syrup,
3 tbsp. lard or shortening,
20 dried lotus seeds,
20 raisins,
8 red dates,
4 candied winter melon,
2 candied small tangerines,
a little of papaya shreds

Procedures

1. Pell off the skin from taro. Cut into 1.5cm thick slices. Steam for about 20 minutes until very tender.
2. Soak the red dates in warm water for about one hour until soft. Remove 4 pieces of pulp from each red date. Soak the dried lotus seeds in warm water for about 3 hours until enlarged. Cut the candied tangerine and winter melon to small pieces.
3. Brush the inside of a mold or bowl with 1 tbsp. lard. Then arrange all of the ingredients except the taro in a pretty design.
4. Mash the steamed taro while it is warm. Place in a bowl with 2/3 cup of syrup and 2 tbsp. lard; mix well. Then put this mixed taro in the mold carefully. Flatten it and cover with a small plate. Steam the pudding for 1 hour. Remove and turn the pudding upside down on a serving platter and serve.

1. 糖漿做法：小鍋中放水 1 1/2 杯、加冰糖 1 杯，用小火熬 20 分鐘，約剩 2/3 杯，即是。
2. 八寶料可以隨自己喜愛挑選使用。

1. If there is no taro, sweet potatoes may be used instead in any of the recipes that call for taro.
2. Any of candied fruit you may use for this recipes; such as, dragon's eyes, cherry, candied red beans.

沙其馬
Sha-Gi-Ma

材料 >>
雞蛋3個、低筋麵粉2 1/2杯、發泡粉2茶匙、麥芽糖150公克、白糖300公克、清水1杯、葡萄乾2大匙、炸油8杯、白芝麻1大匙

做法 >>

1. 將麵粉與發泡粉篩過,放在麵板上,在中間撥開一個凹處,將蛋打下,並用手使勁拌搓揉合,至麵粉成為軟度適當之麵糰。
2. 用擀麵棍將麵糰擀成0.5公分厚之大麵皮形狀,然後切成長約5公分之細麵條狀,全部切好後、撒下乾麵粉拌開(以免黏連在一起)。
3. 將油燒熱後,分3次將切好之麵條投入油中炸黃,然後撈出、瀝乾,裝在大盆內。
4. 在另外小鍋內放下白糖、麥芽糖及清水,用中火熬煮,至糖汁已能拉出絲時,立即離火,馬上淋澆在炸過之麵條中,並速加以拌勻。
5. 將白芝麻炒過與葡萄乾混合,撒在模型中,再將拌過糖漿之麵條全部倒在裡面,用手壓緊,成為約4公分厚,待涼透後再全部切成長塊即成沙其馬。

Ingredients

3 eggs,
2 1/2 cups cake flour,
2 tsp. baking powder,
150g. maltose (or brown sugar),
300g. sugar,
1 cup water,
2 tbsp. raisins,
8 cups oil,
1 tbsp. sesame seeds

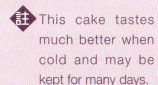

註 This cake tastes much better when cold and may be kept for many days.

Procedures

1. Sift flour and baking powder on the pastry board. Spread to form a hollow in the center. Add eggs. Blend the flour and eggs with fingers. Then knead the dough thoroughly until it is smooth.
2. Roll the dough out with a rolling pin until it is like a big round thin pancake (about 0.5cm thick). Then cut it into 5cm long thin strips. Dust the thin strips with flour, so that they won't stick together.
3. Heat the oil in a pan. Deep fry the thin strips separately until golden brown. Remove, drain and place on a large bowl.
4. In a small sauce pan, add the sugar, maltose and water. boil and stir for a while over low heat until the mixture is sticky like syrup and can be pull out as a thread. Pour it into the fried thin strips and mix thoroughly immediately.
5. Stir fry the white sesame seeds without oil (or roast it lightly). Mix with raisins; sprinkle them on a mold or a deep box. Press No. 4 ingredients on raisins and sesame seeds with palm to form a big square cake, about 4 cm thick. Cut the big cake into pieces with a sharp knife when it gets firmed.

雞蛋撻
Chinese Egg Tart

材料 >>
白糖1杯、開水1 1/4杯、雞蛋5個

油酥料 >>
牛油（或豬油）225公克、低筋麵粉1 1/4杯

水麵料 >>
豬油（或白油）2大匙、中筋麵粉1 3/4杯、雞蛋1個

做法 >>

1. 將牛油放在麵板上，加入麵粉 1 1/4 杯，用手搓拌、揉合成一糰，便是油酥。
2. 將麵粉 1 1/4 杯放在麵板上，中間加入豬油 2 大匙，雞蛋 1 個，用手撥拌、揉搓成一糰，便是水麵（如太硬可稍加一些溫水）。
3. 將油酥及水麵都放入冰箱內，冷藏 15 分鐘左右。
4. 將糖放在大碗內，沖下開水使糖溶化，待糖水冷透後，加入已打散之蛋汁混合，並全部用篩子過濾一次。
5. 由冰箱取出冰鎮的兩塊麵糰，將油酥包進水麵中成一糰，然後放在麵板上，擀開成一大薄片（長方形），折疊兩下（都要相對折），再放入冰箱冰片刻，取出再重擀成 0.6 公分厚的大片。
6. 用壓蛋撻的模型（圓而有波浪邊的）扣壓出一片片的皮子，每一個模型內鋪一片，並用手指壓平，注入第 3 項的蛋汁（8 分滿）。全部排列到烤盤內，再移進預熱好的烤箱中，用 150℃ 烤約 20 分鐘便成。

Ingredients

1 cup sugar,
1 1/4 cups boiling water,
5 eggs

For inside dough

225g. butter or lard or shortening,
1 1/4 cups cake flour

For outside dough

2 tbsp. lard or shortening,
1 3/4 cups all purpose flour,
1 eggs

Procedures

1. Place the ingredients for inside dough on a board and knead them thoroughly. (This is inside layer).
2. Place the ingredients for outside dough on a board; mix them gently into a dough. (This is outside layer).
3. Put two pieces of dough in the refrigerator for about 15 minutes.
4. Add boiling water to the sugar; blend until dissolved. After it gets cold, add the beaten egg and sieve all.
5. Remove the dough from the refrigerator. Wrap the inside dough with the outside dough. Roll it out into a large piece, then fold the dough into quarters (first fold in half and then fold in half again). Then roll it out and fold once more; place in the refrigerator for a while (about 10 minutes). Remove the dough and roll it out to a large piece with 0.6cm thick.
6. Cut the dough with small mold into round pieces. Put each piece in a separate mold. Flatten the bottom with your fingers. Pour the egg mixture into the mold. Place the tarts on a baking tray. Preheat the oven to 250ºF (150℃), bake for 20 minutes.

芝麻鍋炸
Deep-fried Custard Pudding

材料 >>
芝麻3大匙、細白糖4大匙、雞蛋2個、麵粉2/3杯、牛奶水2大匙、水2杯、太白粉1/2杯、炸油6杯

做法 >>

1. 將炒鍋燒熱後,倒下芝麻,用小火炒香。盛出後,待涼透即用擀麵棍擀碎,再加白糖拌勻留用。
2. 在一只大碗內打散雞蛋,加入水及牛奶水,再將麵粉慢慢加入、並調合成稀糊狀(調至無粉粒為止)。
3. 將炒鍋燒熱,倒下已調好之麵糊汁,用炒鏟迅速不停的翻炒拌攪(小火),至煮滾且全部糊汁都已轉成光滑而黏稠之膏狀為止,將鍋離火。
4. 把麵糊膏倒進已塗了麻油的模型中,約1.5公分厚(亦可用便當盒)。待稍冷後,移入冰箱內使其凝固(約2～3小時)。
5. 將已凝固之麵膏(已成塊狀)倒出在板上,先切成1.2公分寬之條狀、再斜切成菱角形,撒上許多太白粉、裹住每一小塊。
6. 在鍋內將炸油燒得極熱之後,分兩次投下上項材料,用大火炸成金黃色為止,撈出後馬上盛碟中,然後撒上第一項之芝麻糖稍拌,即趁熱送食之。

Ingredients

3 tbsp. sesame seeds,
4 tbsp. sugar,
2 eggs,
2/3 cup flour,
2 tbsp. milk,
2 cup cold water,
1/2 cup cornstarch,
6 cups oil

Procedures

1. Heat a pan to very hot. Add sesame seeds; fry for 1 minute over low heat. Don't stop stirring. Remove it after cooling, crush it finely. Mix with sugar in a bowl.
2. Beat the eggs in a large bowl. Then add cold water and milk. Sift flour in; combine them to a smooth paste consistency.
3. Pour the No. 2 flour batter into a pan. Stir fry it over low until it boils and becomes thickened. Turn off the heat.
4. Remove the thickened flour batter (custard like) into a square mold (rub some oil on the mold first). Let cool and remove to the refrigerator for at least 2 hours.
5. Remove the chilled custard from the refrigerator and cut into small diamond shaped pieces. Coat with cornstarch.
6. Deep fry with smoking hot oil for about 1 minute until golden and crispy. Remove and drain; put on a plate. Sprinkle the sesame seed sugar (No. 1) on them. Serve.

 如有雙層鍋(Double Pan)可用上層盛蛋麵汁、而下層鍋盛水去熬煮,則更為理想。
You may use double pan to boil the flour paste.

糯米捲尖
Fried Sweet Rice Pastry

材料 >>
糯米飯3杯、白糖2大匙、豬油2大匙、豆腐衣4張、豆沙1杯、桂花醬少許

做法 >>

1. 將 1 1/2 杯的生糯米加 1 杯水，放入電鍋中煮成約 3 杯的糯米飯。趁糯米飯是熱的時候，加入糖及豬油，仔細調拌均勻，再蒸 10 分鐘左右，使糖及豬油溶在糯米中，增加黏性。
2. 將每張豆腐衣都切成約 12 公分×24 公分的長方形。將糯米飯放到豆腐衣中間，約 4 公分的位置上鋪成一長條（約 4 公分寬），再在糯米飯中間放上一長條豆沙（約 1.5 公分寬），然後蓋上一層糯米飯，覆折豆腐衣兩下、捲壓成寬扁形（厚度僅 0.8 公分），用刀切成 4 公分寬之斜角形（約 6 塊），另外 3 張也相同做好。
3. 將每個切口處沾上乾太白粉少許，排列在燒熱少許油的平底鍋中，用慢火煎黃兩面便成。

Ingredients

3 cups cooked glutinous rice,
2 tbsp. sugar,
2 tbsp. lard or shortening,
4 pieces dried tofu sheet,
1 cup sweet red bean paste

Procedures

1. Add 2 tbsp. sugar and 2 tbsp. lard to the rice while it is still warm. Mix well. Then steam it again for about 10 minutes until the sugar and lard melt.
2. Cut the tofu sheet into 12cm wide, 24cm long pieces. Place 1/8 of rice on each tofu sheet, about 4cm wide from the straight edge (the edge toward you). Put 1/4 amount of the red bean paste on the rice about 1.5cm wide. Then cover with another 1/8 of the rice. Fold the edge twice to make it into a long rectangle about 0.8 cm thick. Cut it into 6cm wide diamond shape pieces. Repeat this process with the other tofu sheets.
3. Dip the cutting sides into cornstarch. Arrange in a heated flat frying pan with some oil. Fry over low heat until both sides are golden brown. Remove to a serving plate.

 如無豆腐衣，可用蛋皮代替。
Instead of tofu sheet, egg sheet may be used.

椰絲糯米球
Glutinous Rice Balls with Coconut Flaker

材料 >>

元宵粉（糯米粉）2 1/2 杯、澄麵（或玉米粉）3 大匙、開水 1/2 杯、豬油 1 大匙、糖 2 大匙、紅豆沙 1 1/2 杯、枸杞子 20 粒、椰子粉 2/3 杯

做法 >>

1. 將元宵粉堆放在麵板上，並在中間撥成一個凹槽，將豬油及糖放在中間。
2. 澄麵另放在小盆中，淋下開水燙熟，並用麵棍或筷子拌成糊狀，然後倒進元宵粉中央，再酌量加入冷水，用手一起拌合揉搓成為軟度適當之一糰（此即是皮子）。
3. 將豆沙平均分成 20 小粒，每一粒都用手搓成圓球狀備用。
4. 把皮子分成 20 小塊，每一小塊中包入豆沙餡一小粒，用雙手搓成小球型，排放在有洞孔的鐵板上（鐵板上要先搽上油），放進蒸籠中。
5. 水開了之後將蒸籠放上，用大火蒸約 7～8 分鐘即熟。趁熱取出後，把外表滾滿椰子粉，排在碟子中，上面再放置一粒泡脹開的枸杞子以增美觀。

Ingredients

2 1/2 cups glutinous rice powder, 3 tbsp. cornstarch, 1/2 cup boiling water, 1 tbsp. lard or shortening, 2 tbsp. sugar, 1 1/2 cups sweet bean paste, 20 pieces medlar, 2/3 cup coconut flakes

Procedures

1. Put the glutinous rice powder on a board. Make a hole in the center. Add sugar and lard in it.
2. Put the cornstarch in a bowl; add boiling water; mix with chop sticks. Pour into glutinous rice powder and knead together. If it is too hard, add some cold water to the dough and knead until very smooth and soft. (This is the wrapper).
3. Divide the sweet bean paste into 20 small round pieces (this is the filling). Soak the medlar to a little soft, drain.
4. Cut the dough into 20 small pieces. Flatten each small piece of dough with the palm of hand. Place 1 piece of sweet bean paste filling (ball shape) in the center of the dough. Pinch and pleat dough, let all the edges come up to top center, so that the dumpling is round. Place all dumplings on a greased steaming board; put it into a steamer.
5. Steam over boiling water with high heat for about 7~8 minutes. Remove and coat with coconut flakes while the dumplings are still very hot. Decorate the top with a piece of medlar; serve.

千層糕

Steamed Thousand Layers Cake

材料 >>
麵粉 3 1/2 杯、酵母粉 2 茶匙、溫水 1 1/2 杯、白糖 1 杯、豬油 1/2 杯、青紅絲（切碎）2 大匙、紅棗（切屑）2 大匙

做法 >>

1. 將酵母粉溶解在 1 1/2 杯的溫水中,之後倒入麵粉內,用手揉合至十分光滑,放置在溫暖處,候其醱酵至 2 倍大(約 3 小時)。
2. 將發好之麵糰移到麵板上,再加揉搓光滑,用麵杖擀成 30 公分長、70 公分寬之薄餅狀,全部塗上一層豬油(用手指或刷子),再將白糖 1 大匙與青紅絲、紅棗等各少許撒在中間 1/3 處。將左邊之麵皮覆蓋向中間,然後也同樣在麵皮上塗上豬油、並撒下 1 大匙糖與少許紅棗屑、青紅絲,再將右邊 1/3 之麵皮覆上。
3. 橫轉一下,再擀成 30 公分長,70 公分寬之薄餅狀,再塗油,撒糖,同樣工作重複做 3 次,最後對折起來,使成為 30 公分長,20 公分寬之大小。放置一旁,待其醒發(約半小時)。
4. 將醒好之千層糕置蒸籠中(籠內應鋪一塊濕白布),用大火蒸約 50 至 60 分鐘。食前分切成小方塊或菱角形即可。

Ingredients

3 1/2 cups flour,
2 tsp. dried yeast,
1 1/2 cups warm water,
1 cup sugar,
1/2 cup lard (or shortening),
2 tbsp. chopped candied papaya shreds,
2 tbsp. chopped red dates

Procedures

1. Place flour in a large bowl. Dissolve yeast with warm water (about 95°C~98°F). Add to flour and knead for about 5 minutes until evenly mixed. Cover with a wet cloth and let it rise until double in bulk.
2. Remove the dough to a pastry board. Knead again until the dough is very smooth. Roll it out until very thin, about 30 cm long, and 70cm wide. Spread some lard and sprinkle 1 tbsp. sugar, soaked red dates and candied papaya over the dough. Fold the right 1/3 portion to cover the middle portion and spread lard, sprinkle sugar, red date and candied papaya on top evenly. Fold the left portion to the center to cover the right portion.
3. Turn the dough around, so that a folded edge face you. Repeat the rolling and spreading procedure twice. Finally fold the dough into 30cm long and 20cm wide. Let the cake rest for 30 minutes.
4. Place the cake on a wet cloth in a steamer. Place over boiling water; steam for about 50 to 60 minutes. Remove and let cool a little. Cut into small squares or diamonds. Serve.

培梅食譜
《第二冊》

作　　者	傅培梅
發 行 人	程安琪
總 策 劃	程顯灝
編　　輯	陳霓瑩
攝　　影	張志銘
封面設計	洪瑞伯
美術設計	徐正懿
出 版 者	橘子文化事業有限公司
地　　址	110 台北市信義路3段3號7樓之1
電　　話	02-27556977
傳　　真	02-27006439
E-mail	service@sanyau.com.tw
總 代 理	三友圖書有限公司
地　　址	台北縣中和市中山路二段327巷11弄17號5樓
電　　話	(02)22405600
傳　　真	(02)22409284
E-MAIL	sanyau@sanyau.com.tw
郵政劃撥	05844889 三友圖書有限公司
總 經 銷	貿騰發賣股份有限公司
地　　址	台北縣中和市中正路880號14樓
電　　話	02-22313503
傳　　真	02-22313384
初　　版	2005年9月
定　　價	新臺幣 450 元
Ｉ Ｓ Ｂ Ｎ	986-7997-63-8（精裝）

國家圖書館出版預行編目資料

培梅食譜 / 傅培梅著. -- 初版. -- 台北市：
橘子. 2005〔民94〕 —
　　冊：　公分
　　中英對照
　　　ISBN 986-7997-33-6 (第1冊：精裝). --
　　　ISBN 986-7997-63-8 (第2冊：精裝)

1. 食譜 — 中國

427.11　　　　　　　　　　93000690

◎版權所有・翻印必究◎
書若有破損缺頁請請寄回本社更換

廣　告　回　函
臺灣北區郵政管理局登記證
北 台 字 第　7945　號

地址：　　　縣/市　　　鄉/鎮/市/區　　　路/街

段　　巷　　弄　　號　　樓

三友圖書有限公司 收

235 中和市中山路二段327巷11弄17號5樓

三友圖書
讀者特惠區

為了感謝三友圖書忠實讀者，只要您詳細填寫背面問卷，並郵寄給我們，即可**免費獲贈1套價值320元**的《**夢幻蔬菜料理**》。

請勾選

☐ 我不需要這本書

☐ 我想索取這本書（回函時請附80元郵票，做為郵寄費用）

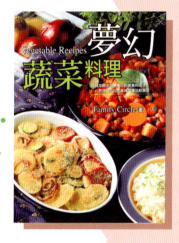

我購買了 **培梅食譜 II**

❶ 個人資料

姓名 _____ 出生 ____ 年 ____ 月 ____ 日 教育程度 _____ 職業 _____

傳真 _____

電話 _____ 電子信箱 _____

❷ 您想免費索取三友書訊嗎？ □需要（請提供電子信箱帳號）　□不需要

❸ 您大約什麼時間購買本書？ _____ 年 _____ 月 _____ 日

❹ 您從何處購買此書？ _____ 縣市 _____ 書店／量販店

　　□書展 □郵購 □網路 □其他

❺ 您從何處得知本書的出版？

　　□書店 □報紙 □雜誌 □書訊 □廣播 □電視 □網路 □親朋好友 □其他

❻ 您購買這本書的原因？（可複選）

　　□對主題有興趣 □生活上的需要 □工作上的需要 □出版社 □作者

　　□價格合理（如果不合理，您覺得合理價錢應 _____ ）

　　□除了食譜以外，還有許多豐富有用的資訊

　　□版面編排 □拍照風格 □其他

❼ 您最常在什麼地方買書？

　　_____ 縣市 _____ 書店／量販店

❽ 您希望我們未來出版何種主題的食譜書？

❾ 您經常購買哪類主題的食譜書？（可複選）

　　□中菜 □中式點心 □西點 □歐美料理（請說明）_____

　　□日本料理 □亞洲料理（請說明）_____

　　□飲料冰品 □醫療飲食（請說明）_____

　　□飲食文化 □烹飪問答集 □其他

❿ 您最喜歡的食譜出版社？（可複選）

　　□橘子 □旗林 □二魚 □三采 □大境 □台視文化 □生活品味

　　□朱雀 □邦聯 □楊桃 □積木 □暢文 □躍昇 □膳書房 □其他

⓫ 您購買食譜書的考量因素有哪些？

　　□作者 □主題 □攝影 □出版社 □價格 □實用 □其他 _____

⓬ 除了食譜書外，您希望本社另外出版哪些書籍？

　　□健康 □減肥 □美容 □飲食文化 □DIY書籍 □其他 _____

⓭ 您認為本書尚需改進之處？以及您對我們的建議？ _____

懷念 傅老師的心情再版發行

傅培梅時間

美味台菜
書系 流行美食 書號08
開本 25.5X21公分
頁數128 定價 350元
作者 傅培梅、程安琪

【內容簡介】
出自閩菜源流之台菜，由於受到日本菜、客家菜及粵菜的薰陶，自成一格，發展出鮮香、清淡的特性。除了海鮮、冷盤、生食外，湯湯水水更是一大特色。在本書中，也詳盡介紹了酒家菜、辦桌〔喜宴、壽宴、喬遷宴〕，小吃也有數百種以上。

培梅食譜第一冊
書系 培梅食譜 書號01
開本 19.3x21.3公分
頁數 365 定價 500元
作者 傅培梅

【內容簡介】
這本培梅食譜，是台灣最早的一本彩色且中英對照食譜，至今已近40個年頭，陪伴了許多中外人士從青年、壯年、一直到老年。也因為傅老師對傳承中華美食的努力，使得中國菜能在世界各地留下真正的文字與圖片紀錄。

五味八珍的歲月傅培梅傳
開本 21x15公分
頁數 224 定價 158元
作者 傅培梅

【內容簡介】
傅培梅女士，中國第一位將中華美食帶到全世界的偉大女性，您知道她是如何從一個完全不懂做菜，卻在婚後為了家庭開始走進廚房，而後竟成為全世界家喻戶曉的中華美食大師，中間的過程絕對會讓您感動萬分！

培梅創意家常菜
書系 家庭化系列 書號03
開本 21x25.5公分
頁數 144 定價 400元
作者 傅培梅、程安琪

【內容簡介】
以簡單、容易買到的材料，做出家人愛吃的家常菜，當親朋好友聚會時，也做得出色香味俱全的宴客菜，讓擅長與不善料理的人都能呈現出拿手好菜。飲食雖然有流行趨勢，但好吃的味道是永遠令人垂涎嚮往的，全部中英對照，無論自用、贈送外籍友人，皆相當適用。

培梅家常菜
書系 流行美食 書號04
開本 21x25.5公分
頁數 144 定價 400元
作者 傅培梅、程安琪

【內容簡介】
出版20年、銷售超過六十萬冊堪稱最長壽且銷售最好的食譜，且為了因應時代的進步、飲食習慣的改變，特將"培梅家常菜"重新改版，以適應現代國人的飲食習慣，更加入了中英對照，以配合現代許多有外籍傭人的家庭，以期造福更多的家庭與傳承中華美食。

懷念 傅老師的心情再版發行

傅培梅時間

2600道菜 集結成冊

書名 傅培梅時間 III
書系 美食大師 書號07
開本 19x25.5公分
頁數126 定價 320元
作者 傅培梅

書名 傅培梅時間 I
書系 美食大師 書號05
開本 19x25.5公分
頁數 126 定價 320元
作者 傅培梅

書名 傅培梅時間 V
書系 美食大師 書號09
開本 19x25.5公分
頁數 126 定價 320元
作者 傅培梅

書名 傅培梅時間 II
書系 美食大師 書號06
開本 19x25.5公分
頁數126 定價 320元
作者 傅培梅

書名 傅培梅時間 IV
書系 美食大師 書號08
開本 19x25.5公分
頁數 126 定價 320元
作者 傅培梅